Stop Thinking About It:

Why Your Brain Won't Shut Up – And How To Finally Quiet It

by Nick Trenton

www.NickTrenton.com

Table of Contents

Introduction

What is overthinking?

That's simple: A trapped mind.

Overthinking is so much more than just "thinking too much."

It's not merely an excess of ordinary cognitive processes, but an entirely distinct mental phenomenon—a *way* of thinking which creates traps, snares, and mazes for the mind to fall into.

Are you an overthinker?

- You find yourself endlessly dwelling, rehashing, rehearsing, remembering, dissecting, investigating, predicting, listing, arguing, worrying... and you can't seem to stop.
- You keep replaying mistakes, embarrassments, and awkward moments in your mind on loop.
- Your mind keeps returning to the same old worries, and each time they get just a little bigger, a little scarier, a little more overwhelming...

- **You** often get so stuck in second-guessing, analysis, "research", and planning that you feel too paralyzed to make *any* decision.
- **Life** feels tense, negative, and gloomy. You're on edge and can't relax even when you've done everything right.
- **You** regularly stew over life's big meaty questions, but nothing actually changes in your world—except that you keep yourself up at night and wake up with a headache!

If you've had enough of overthinking and what it's costing you, you've come to the right place. **This book is designed to help you untangle the anxiety knot and break free from the trap of overthinking, once and for all.**

Through the chapters that follow, we'll learn exactly what overthinking is, how it functions, and how we can make evidence-based, practical changes that bring us closer to real peace and wellbeing, every single day.

We'll begin with approaches and methods that have **sound scientific evidence** to support their efficacy, then find creative ways to start applying those principles in our own lives, starting from today.

- In Chapter 1, we discover the basic misunderstanding that lies at the heart of almost all overthinking—and how things change when we **start telling a different story.**

- In Chapter 2, we learn something surprising—that overthinking *works*. But we'll also start **building a whole new skill set** that works much, much better than overthinking ever could.
- In Chapter 3, we see that the solution to overthinking is not *no* thinking, it's better thinking. We explore in detail what healthy thinking actually looks like, and how we can start to **make concrete changes to our thinking style.**
- In Chapter 4, once we've laid the groundwork, we dig a little deeper to find out **how to restructure our minds** so that overthinking is simply no longer a part of our lives.
- And finally, in Chapter 5, we see why winning the war against anxiety means choosing never to fight in the first place… and **what to do instead.**

There are no shortcuts or cheat codes in life.

However, when it comes to anxious overthinking, we don't need any—because the best way out is through slow, consistent, and *gentle* shifts, one day at a time.

With patience, self-compassion, and a little willingness to try something different, you can slowly—but powerfully—dismantle the engine of overthinking, and start living a life of balance, stability, and joy.

Ready to get started?

Chapter One – The Overthinking Mind

No two overthinkers are the same.

Anxiety looks different for everyone, and even for the same person it can feel different from one day to the next.

Broadly speaking, overthinking flows from and is sustained by a **mindset of distorted threat detection:**

- "Anxious sensations are dangerous."
- "My thoughts are uncontrollable."
- "Ambiguity is a threat."

Once we learn to dismantle these and other default "doom associations" that have been controlling our thought processes, we can start making *new* interpretations—ones that help us feel grounded and at ease.

Reduce the "anxious sensations are dangerous" response

"He who fears he will suffer, already suffers because he fears."

\-   *Michel de Montaigne*

Big idea: Anxiety sensitivity is the tendency to interpret neutral sensations as dangerous, and it can set up vicious cycles of anxiety. Breaking that cycle isn't about stopping the sensation. It's about changing the interpretation.

So... what's making you anxious?

- Other people?
- Ambiguous situations?
- Awkward social scenarios?
- Pressures and triggers?
- Uncertainty?

In this first chapter, we'll consider things from another angle—that the real cause of your anxiety might nothing to do with these things.

Rather, your anxiety might stem from the *reaction* you are having to anxiety-related sensations.

"Anxiety sensitivity" is often called a "fear of fear".

But this is not entirely accurate. **Anxiety sensitivity is really a reaction to a *belief* we have about certain sensations.**

Consider the sensation of a *racing heart*:

- The belief about that sensation – "Something dangerous is happening to me physically."
- The result – MORE FEAR

Or, consider the experience of *sweating and blushing*:

- The meaning ascribed to that sensation – "People will see and judge me."
- The result – MORE FEAR

Or the feeling of *dizziness or light-headedness*:

- The interpretation given to that sensation – "I must be losing my mind. I'm going crazy."
- The result – MORE FEAR

In each case, the sensation is certainly real, but it's *neutral*.

The sensation *itself* isn't causing the reaction.

The story we tell ourselves about the sensation is what's causing the reaction.

Anxiety sensitivity acts like a magnifying glass—or a fun house mirror! It takes genuine sensations and *amplifies* and *distorts* them into something that isn't genuine.

And what happens then? More fear.

Unsurprisingly, anxiety sensitivity plays a big role in the development of anxiety disorders like panic attacks, PTSD, and OCD. While most people understand that this pattern is a *symptom* of anxiety, what's more important is to understand that it's also a *cause* of that anxiety.

Anxiety sensitivity is thus a cause and an effect.

- ➜ You feel a sensation
- ➜ You tell yourself, "This sensation is dangerous"
- ➜ You feel afraid

→ That fear produces heightened sensations

→ You experience that sensation *even more strongly*

→ You tell yourself, "The danger is increasing"

→ And on and on...

Looking through the magnifying glass of anxiety sensitivity, even the smallest sensation can be blown into catastrophic proportions.

So how do we break this vicious cycle?

- **One** answer that anxiety-sufferers sometimes give is: "I have to stop myself from blushing/slow down my heart rate/stop feeling dizzy."

But this line of reasoning is a trap.

Why? Because it confirms the belief that the sensation is dangerous in the first place. And it isn't!

The actual problem:

The **interpretation** of the sensation.

The **beliefs** about that sensation.

The **meaning** we give to the sensation.

The truth is that we are not always in control of our physiological sensations.

- Sometimes, we'll feel dizzy, blush, or become aware of our hearts racing.

- Sometimes, we'll feel anxious, panicked, or get that weird queasy feeling in the pit of our stomachs.
- Sometimes we'll be in a social situation and realize that our hands are shaking or our voice is quivering.

While we can't necessarily control these things, we **can** control the interpretations, beliefs, and meaning we attach to each experience.

Anxiety sensitivity is the "**fear of anxiety-related sensations**" (McNally, 2002). The anxious mind takes a seed of truth and blows it up into a catastrophic lie.

That means that anxiety sensitivity is not "all in your head." The sensation you feel is real.

You really are sweating, and your heart really is beating faster.

But what does it all *mean*?

- "I'm lightheaded, so I must be having a stroke."
- "I'm blushing, so that means public shame and humiliation."
- "I'm shaking, so I must be having nervous breakdown."

The sensations are real… but the interpretation is pretty warped.

Psychologists term these sensations "arousal."

Arousal simply means a whole-body state of *activation*. It's a condition of physiological stimulation, and psychological awareness and readiness.

Importantly, **arousal sensations are neither good nor bad.** They're just something your body is doing.

Consider:

- "I'm lightheaded because I'm trying something new and I'm a little nervous."
- "I'm blushing because I'm feeling some social discomfort, but I'm not in any danger."
- "I'm shaking because I'm excited and alert."

The fascinating thing is that this principle applies to any sensation—including mental and psychological ones. **We can learn to re-interpret *any* experience, whether psychological, cognitive, or physical:**

- "My thoughts are not dangerous."
- "My feelings are not dangerous."
- "My physical sensations and perceptions are not dangerous."

In a 2007 study in the Journal of Anxiety Disorders, (Schmidt, N. B., et al., 2007), researchers were interested in finding out whether people could be trained to change the way they interpreted their own bodily sensations.

In other words, **could people learn to lower their anxiety sensitivity?**

The encouraging answer is that yes, they could!

First, the researchers picked around 400 participants they knew had high anxiety sensitivity by getting them to complete a test (the Anxiety Sensitivity Index—ASI).

- Some of these they assigned to a group that would take part in a training program.
- Some of these they assigned to a control group—they would not complete any training.

After completing the computer-based Anxiety Sensitivity Amelioration Training, there was a follow-up at 24 months to see if their results had stuck.

The training group showed promising reductions in anxiety sensitivity—reductions that the control group didn't show.

Overall, the authors concluded that directly targeting anxiety sensitivity was a powerful way to prevent the development of anxiety disorders and other Axis I pathology (episodic or acute disorders).

The verdict is simple: By reducing anxiety sensitivity, we lower our risk of experiencing episodic mental conditions.

Though we do not have access to the computer-based training program the researchers used in their study, the good news is that we don't need to—there are several DIY techniques that anyone can use in their everyday lives.

One especially useful one is outlined below.

How to dial down reactivity

Step 1: Name the loop + name the normal cause

First, notice when things suddenly feel urgent, panicky, or intense.

Notice the spike in emotion, the flutters of physiological arousal, the sudden increase in mental activity.

Then just pause.

Take a moment, aware and present.

At this point, you can choose: Let the vicious cycle run through again and again, or decide not to board that ride.

Instead:

1. Name the loop
2. Name the "normal cause"

You don't have to gaslight yourself into thinking that you are not really experiencing what you're experiencing.

You are.

And that's OK.

Your work will take place in the meaning you assign. Try to get curious about the story you're telling, and if there is a healthier, more reasonable story you could tell instead.

- **Physical reactivity**
  - o Name the loop: "I can feel my heartbeat. I'm worried that means something is wrong with me. That scary thought is making my heart beat even faster."
  - o Name the normal cause: "My heartbeat is responding to what it thinks is a genuine alarm and is trying to help keep me safe."
  - → The sensation is *uncomfortable, but not dangerous.*
- **Psychological reactivity**
  - o Name the loop: "I am aware of some very big, confusing emotions right now. I feel like this means I'm going crazy. That makes everything feel more overwhelming and terrifying."
  - o Name the normal cause: "My emotions are spinning out of control because they're trying to help me make sense of the situation."
  - → The situation is *confusing and uncertain, but not dangerous.*
- **Cognitive reactivity**
  - o Name the loop: "I keep coming back to the same stressful thought, but the more I think of it, the more stressed I'm getting."
  - o Name the normal cause: "This is my brain searching for certainty or closure."

→ This situation is *unpleasant and unresolved, but not dangerous.*

The point here is not to run away from your sensations, fix them, or come up with a clever-sounding explanation for them.

In fact, the first thing you want to do is simply *normalize* them.

It's NOT the end of the world.

It's NOT proof that something is going wrong.

It's NOT a sign that something dangerous is happening.

You may be feeling hot and nervous because you're in a sauna. Or maybe it's because your mind is lingering on an embarrassing memory.

Whatever it is, you don't have to argue away the existence of this horrible sensation—you just have to accept that that's all it is—a sensation.

Not a danger, not a serious and genuine threat to your survival, not an emergency.

Does it feel good? Nope! In fact, it can feel *really* awkward and uncomfortable and weird.

But it's not dangerous.

Remind yourself of that.

That's the first step.

Step 2: Practice a little micro-tolerance

The next step is to set a timer for two minutes and *let the overthinking loop run* without fixing it.

How did you feel when you read that sentence?

"Let the loop just run? Why would I do *that*!?"

It feels like a dangerous thing to do.

And that's exactly why step 2 is so important—because it teaches you that, well, it isn't a dangerous thing to do at all. It's an *uncomfortable* thing... but a thing you can learn to comfortably tolerate.

Practicing tolerance isn't meant to be a big grueling punishment. Just start small and practice "sitting with" your discomfort for a little while. That's all.

Keep telling yourself, "I'm still here."

Then what happens?

- You learn that you can have repetitive thoughts without obeying them or reacting automatically or impulsively to them.
- You learn that you can endure uncomfortable or unpleasant physical sensations without anything bad happening.
- You learn that you can experience emotions—even big ones—without needing to escape.

In the moment, that might not feel like much. But the next time that this feeling comes around, you might feel a little different about it.

Like it's not quite so urgent as it used to be.

Like it's not quite as big a deal as you thought previously.

And that's real progress. It means that you've loosened the grip that anxiety has over you. The wonderful thing is that you don't need to force positivity, pretend, or rush in to try and push any experience to be something it isn't.

You just have to gently shift your perception *around* that experience.

- Old interpretation: "My anxious experience is dangerous."
- New interpretation: "I can have anxious experiences without it being unsafe."

Talk kindly to yourself:

- "I don't like experiencing anxiety, but it's OK that I am experiencing it."
- "These sensations are normal. I don't have to react."
- "I'm safe, even if it doesn't feel like it right now."
- "This experience is temporary."

Let go of "I can't control my thinking"

"My experience is what I agree to attend to. Only those items I notice shape my mind."

- *William James*

Big idea: Anxiety worsens when you believe you are helpless and at its mercy. Instead, adopt a mindset where you focus on what you

can control, and take action—even if it's only small.

Our next investigation is into the now-classic study first published in the *Archives of General Psychiatry* in the late 1980s (Sanderson, et. al.,1989).

In this study, the researchers recruited twenty patients who had been diagnosed with panic disorder, and then they issued them an unusual "physiological challenge"—they had them inhale 5.5% carbon-dioxide enriched air for a full 15 minutes.

Why?

Because it's a safe, controlled, and reliable method of artificially inducing anxiety.

When there is slightly too much CO2 in the air you breathe, the brain can trigger a kind of "false suffocation alarm"—and this *physiological* arousal is naturally associated with *psychological* states of panic.

In this way, psychiatric researchers can model and study anxiety directly in the laboratory.

Now, a 5.5% concentration is pretty mild—in fact, it's pretty much the definition of "uncomfortable but not dangerous." It's a fairly neutral physiological sensation that may be interpreted catastrophically: "I have shortness of breath because I'm dying!"

Here's where the study got interesting:

"All patients were instructed that illumination of a light directly in front of them would signal that they could decrease the amount of CO2 that they were receiving, if desired, by turning a dial attached to their chair. For ten patients, the light was illuminated during the entire administration of CO2. For the remaining ten patients, the light was never illuminated. In fact, all patients experienced the full CO2 mixture, and the dial was ineffective."

To summarize:

- Ten patients were led to believe they **could control** the CO2 levels (and therefore control the panic sensation).
- Ten of the patients were led to believe that they **couldn't control** CO2 levels (because the light that would allow them to do so never went on).

How did these groups compare?

When compared to the first group, subjects in the second group:

- Reported a higher number of panic-attack symptoms.
- Rated the intensity of those symptoms higher.
- Had higher reported claims of subjective anxiety.
- Reported thinking more catastrophic thoughts.

The key detail here is that every person in the study inhaled the *same* CO2 concentration, and each of them had the *same* degree of control over the situation—that is, none (the control dial did nothing).

What does this tell us?

➜ **Your perception of control changes how intensely you experience internal panic alarms.**

Put another way, the beliefs about the control you have over a situation influence how you interpret that situation.

This makes sense—if you believe that a risky or unpleasant situation will respond to your influence, you may feel less at its mercy. *Your catastrophic rumination drops as your perceived competence increases.*

"This situation is pretty bad. But I can do things to improve it."

The radical idea here is that the subjects who believed they had control of the situation experienced *precisely the same stress trigger.*

Imagine how a subject might have felt a little panicked, then reached for the dial to turn down the CO2 concentration. Then they felt less anxious.

However, *the dial did nothing. The CO2 level stayed exactly the same.*

So, what made them less anxious?

- The **action** of taking control of the situation.
- The expression of their **agency**.
- Their attempt to shape the situation, and their **confident expectation** that they could do so.

For those of us who suffer from anxiety, this result should blow our minds. It gives plain evidence that **our perception directly impacts the anxiety we feel.**

Certain beliefs are so powerful that they can effectively cancel out the physiological effect of high CO_2 levels.

So how can we use this insight practically in our own lives?

How to increase perceived control

When you don't think you have a choice in how a **situation** unfolds, that situation is bound to feel scarier.

Maybe when you read the above you immediately **thought,** "But wait, I *don't* have a choice in this awful situation!"

There's the key!

→ You don't have to have a choice.
→ You only have to have a *perceived* choice.

Recall that the people in the study had 0% control **over the** situation. The only variable was their *belief* in their level of control.

Does this mean that you have to try and fool yourself?

Thankfully, no.

But it does mean that **you can seriously dampen anxiety feelings by simply dwelling in the frame of mind that focuses on what you can control.**

The power of control here lies not in what you can actually do, but in the *action* you take, the *agency* you claim for yourself, and the *confident expectation* that you are not a passive victim at the mercy of your own life, but an active player who can make choices.

When it comes to overthinking, one of the most debilitating stories we tell ourselves is that we aren't in charge, and that our overthinking is entirely out of our control.

But that thought alone intensifies feelings of anxiety!

The truth is that you *are* in charge.

You can steer your mind.

Step 1: Make a "steering wheel menu"

Remember:

- You have a say in how your life goes.
- You are not doomed to sit powerlessly while anxiety happens to you.
- You can *do* things.

What things?

When you're feeling clam and grounded, take a few moments to write down some simple and easy actions that you can take to gently derail an anxiety spiral when it does hit.

Aim for around five actions or so, for example:

1. Get up and move/stretch for 60 seconds.
2. Make a cup of tea or get a glass of water to sip for a moment.
3. Write one line in your journal.
4. Do one tiny task, like tidying the book pile on your desk or cleaning your glasses.
5. Splash water on your face or put on some scented hand lotion.

These little tasks are kind of meaningless in themselves, but they do something very important: They get you into an *active* frame of mind. They remind you that *no matter what, you have choices*—you can act to improve your situation, even if that situation feels difficult.

Step 2: When anxiety hits, pick one action

When you start to feel yourself spiraling, go back to your steering wheel and pick one task to do, even if all you can manage is 60 seconds.

You might like to pair this action with supportive affirmations that drive home that *active, choosing* mindset:

- "I can't control what pops up, but I can control what I do next."

- "I am in charge of my peace."
- "The future is not pre-destined. I can shape it."

Important caveat: "Taking control" doesn't mean going into resistance or fearful force. It doesn't mean anxiously trying to fix the problem, or spiraling into blame, judgment, and condemnation. In fact, the action you take does not even need to be connected to your current anxiety.

Instead, it's enough to simply take action, while you tell yourself, "I'm in charge. I'm doing something. I'm in control."

You always have the power to change your mindset.

You always have the power to shift where your attention is going.

And you always have the power to choose one thought over another, one action over another.

It doesn't matter how you reconnect to that power, only that you reconnect to it.

Retrain the "ambiguity = danger" bias

"Maturity of mind is the capacity to endure uncertainty."

- *John Finley*

Big idea: People who tend to interpret ambiguous situations as threatening are more likely to experience anxiety and panic. Rather than endlessly overthinking the "threat,"

however, we can reappraise the interpretation that labelled this experience as a threat in the first place.

For many people, anxiety feels like it makes a kind of obvious sense. We don't really question it.

We respond to a situation automatically, and in a way that never really leaves any space for alternatives.

The unconscious logic goes a little like this: *"I wouldn't be feeling so worried and anxious unless there was something to be scared of, right?"*

In other words, we think:

- Event → Response

Without reflecting on it too much, we assume that we are responding with fear and apprehension to a situation because... well, that situation *is* threatening:

- Threatening event → Fearful response

Often, however, the picture looks more like this:

- Event → Interpretation → Response

Even though it may not feel like, we're often responding not to the situation itself, but to *our own story about what that situation means*:

- Event → Interpretation of event as threatening → Fearful response

Example: You message an invitation to a newish friend. Four hours later they still haven't replied.

That's the event.

"Maybe they don't want to come but they're avoiding replying because they don't want to hurt my feelings."

That's the interpretation.

This interpretation turns the event into a threat, and the response is only natural: You feel anxious and unsettled.

Now this isn't to say that feeling panicked, uneasy, or afraid is somehow wrong. Note above that fear is the correct response to something that *genuinely* threatens us.

The problem is not in the response itself, but in the inappropriate interpretation (it would, after all, be just as inappropriate to interpret a dangerous situation as non-threatening—but readers of this book are likely not affected by *this* bias!).

Let's go a little further. Bias happens not when we confuse what is genuinely threatening with what isn't. Usually, that's pretty clear—few of us mistake ice cream cones and kittens as genuine threats to life.

Biased interpretation is a little subtler and harder to see. Rather than interpreting safe situations as dangerous, we tend to do something else: **We interpret *ambiguous* situations as threatening.**

An ambiguous situation is tricky precisely because it's *not* clear whether it's good or bad, dangerous or safe.

We simply don't know.

Biased interpretation has us take that "I don't know" and round it up to, "it's bad."

We may do this so quickly that we genuinely believe it *is* a dangerous situation, and we're simply responding in an obvious and rational way.

Once we truly understand the power that we hold to favor certain interpretations over others, we can appreciate the implications:

→ Even though we perceive a threat, and even though our inbuilt alarm system may be strongly set off, it doesn't automatically follow that there is a threat.

As you can imagine, a bias for seeing threats where there aren't any is strongly correlated with anxiety.

A 2014 study (Woud et. al., 2014) gives compelling evidence that people with a "threat-leaning interpretation" were more likely to have developed a panic disorder when assessed later on (17 months later, in this study). This was the case even if a participant didn't have a panic disorder to start with!

The researchers concluded that **this kind of interpretative bias was so reliably predictive of future panic disorder that they considered it a**

risk factor (along with, interestingly, anxiety sensitivity).

Understanding why isn't rocket science. If your perception routinely creates more for you to fear, then it's no surprise that your life will soon be dominated by panic.

You may waste enormous amounts of time and energy ruminating over, planning for, avoiding, and analyzing situations that don't actually exist.

This bias runs deep. Really deep.

It is the unconscious belief that:

- We do know everything.
- We can know everything.
- We *should* know everything.

You only need to pause for a second to see how unrealistic this really is.

Do you *really* know everything that is going on inside another person's heart and mind?

Do you *really* understand all the events, the causes and effects, and the countless complicated circumstances unfolding this very minute in the world around you?

Do you *really* know everything that will happen tomorrow? Or the day after that?

Uncertainty is a part of life.

The portion of reality that we can clearly see, control, predict, understand, or explain is *vastly* smaller than the portion we can't.

But this in itself isn't a problem. **It's only when we interpret all this ambiguity and uncertainty as threatening that we create the problem of anxiety.**

It's as though the anxious mind is not content with "I don't know" and would *prefer to know*—even if it has to make something up. So it forces a conclusion, and that conclusion is almost always a negative one.

Every single day you may encounter dozens upon dozens of ambiguous or uncertain situations:

- Your boss has asked for an update on a new assignment she's given you, but her instructions were pretty vague and you don't understand exactly what she means by an "update" anyway.
- You suggested a place for dinner this evening and your partner said, "I don't know, can I think about it?" but they still haven't given you an answer yet.
- You gave a family member an extravagant birthday gift and they said, "Ooh, I could just kill you, this is way too much!" and now you're concerned that they're actually serious and hate your gift.
- You see a young, unaccompanied child in the park on your lunch break. Later, you're feeling a bit guilty, and can't stop wondering

whether there was a problem, and you should have done something.

- You walk past an acquaintance in the street, and they frown when they see you... but quickly smile when you greet them. Now you feel weird.

What do any of these situations *mean*?

Which situation is a genuine problem, and which is probably fine?

Which scenario contains potential threat?

Here's the core of the issue: **We don't know.**

We might get to find out later, or we may gain partial clarity in time...

...or we may *never* know.

How does a healthy person respond to this inconvenient and uncomfortable truth?

Sometimes, instead of jumping to negative conclusions, we do the opposite; we try to reassure ourselves by forcing a *positive* interpretation on an ambiguous situation:

- "I'm sure my acquaintance just didn't recognize me, that's why they frowned. They probably think I'm great. Everything's fine."
- "The child's parents were most likely nearby; you just didn't see them. It's nothing."
- "My partner is just taking their time making a decision about dinner. It's a good sign—it shows how much they care."

But can you see the problem here?

The "positive" interpretation is *still* a bias—and **seeking reassurance still betrays an intolerance for uncertainty.**

Guess what that means?

It means you're still interpreting ambiguity as a threat.

Remember, it's not the response that matters, but whether that response is truly, genuinely appropriate for the situation that triggered it.

"But how do I know how to respond if I don't know how threatening the situation actually is?!"

And there it is again—*you don't*.

The maturity and the discipline comes in being able to acknowledge that.

So, what *is* the most appropriate response to an uncertain or ambiguous situation?

- "I don't know." (Not, "I don't know but I'm going to guess or tell myself a story about what I wish/fear is the case." Just, "I don't know").
- "I don't have a lot of information right now so I'm not going to make a pronouncement either way. I don't have to have an opinion or respond at all."
- "I may know more later. I'm comfortable with waiting. A delay is not a threat."

- "I don't have to have all the answers to make a good decision now or take the next right step. I can figure things out as I go."
- "This is a process. Today I'll engage with today's business, and I'll deal with tomorrow's business tomorrow."
- "I understand I'm not always in complete control, and I don't need to be to feel safe."
- "I don't need to predict the future to be well-prepared for it. I can do my best in this moment, and that is enough."
- "I can rest, even if there are still some things unresolved in my world."

We are cultivating **ambiguity tolerance.**

According to Else Frenkel-Brunswik (1949), this is the ability to handle situations without needing immediate, rigid, black-and-white answers.

- **High Tolerance:** I can be comfortable with:

  - Change

  - Novelty

  - Complexity

  - Delay

- **Low Tolerance:** I cannot bear uncertainty and prefer:

  - Rigid rules

  - Immediate closure / certainty

  - Things that are familiar

By cultivating high ambiguity tolerance, we are programming new beliefs:

→ Ambiguity is not dangerous.
→ I do not need rigidity, familiarity, and certainty to feel safe.
→ I can be uncomfortable in the face of the unknown.

How to change the story you tell about ambiguity

Interpretation bias leads to overthinking.

When you tell a story to fill in the black hole of the unknown, that story can theoretically go on and on. Soon you're telling stories about the story, and your emotional responses are generating more emotional responses.

The trick to catching anxious overthinking before it gets to this place is to focus your attention on the *interpretation* you're giving—not on the resulting *response* you're experiencing.

By the time you're anxious and spiraling, it may already be too late. You have told yourself that there is a threat, and your inbuilt self-preservation mechanisms have been activated to deal with that threat.

IMPORTANT: There's little point arguing with this response, judging it, or, as we've seen, trying to reassure it. In fact, try not to engage with your own panic at all, and keep turning your attention elsewhere: to your interpretation of this event.

Here are some ways you can do that.

Technique 1: "Three stories"

OK. So you're overthinking.

You're anxious.

You're feeling strung out or on edge about something.

Your mind is circling and you feel like you're trapped in a sinking pit and can't pull yourself out.

> "Why were they so rude about my gift? What's so wrong with my gifts, anyway? Why are people like this? I should never have bothered. I don't know why I let myself get taken for granted like this. People don't appreciate me and I'm sick of it..."

See this? This is what it looks like to *engage* with anxiety. You've taken your interpretation as a given and then run with it.

This exercise asks you to do something different: Play around with different interpretations, and see how that changes the way you think and feel.

Try to set your feelings aside for a moment, and tell yourself three different stories, that is, three alternative interpretations:

- **Story 1:** Worst case scenario.
- **Story 2:** Neutral or boring interpretation.
- **Story 3:** The "likely OK" explanation.

In our example:

- **Story 1:** "Everyone hates me and nobody appreciates what I do for them."
- **Story 2:** "My relative said what she did without thinking, and it doesn't mean anything. She neither loves nor hates my gift, and her response was nothing personal."
- **Story 3:** "She likes my gift but was surprised at the expense and expressed this surprise a little clumsily."

The next thing you're going to do is *consciously choose to believe either Story 2 or Story 3.*

Then you're going to file the issue away in your mind and do your best to move on.

Note: You don't have to tell yourself a "best-case scenario" story and you don't have to bend over backwards to reassure yourself. Chances are,

a)   It's probably not completely true, and
b)   You wouldn't really buy it anyway, right?

"Neutral" or "fine" are perfectly good replacements for the worst-case scenario!

Technique 2: Counter with affirmations

When you're already spiraling, your interpretation has been taken as gospel truth and your physical and psychological "threat program" is in full swing.

But you can take a moment to write down some conscious alternatives before you get to this point. Then, when you notice your mind starting to run away with you, you can reach for this "alternative script."

You might still feel somewhat anxious, but just reminding yourself of plausible alternatives can change things.

→ You are reminding yourself that you are not necessarily responding to reality, but to your interpretation of reality. And there are other interpretations…

You could write these alternatives on a sticky note or use a Notes app on your phone so you can reach for them in an emergency.

Let's say one day you catch yourself thinking, "Why did that person frown at me in the street? Are they angry at me? Have I done something wrong? Could I have done something really bad and don't even know about it?"

Reach for your notes, and re-read your affirmations:

- "There is no problem or danger. I just don't have enough information."
- "There is nothing for me to figure out or do. I'm safe."
- "I don't know. And I can leave it at that."

Keep returning to your notes until the peak of anxiety passes.

Change the automatic "doom feeling" attached to your thoughts

"If you change the way you look at things, the things you look at change."

\-   *Wayne Dyer*

Big idea: Cognitive change comes before symptom change. Before we can reduce anxiety, we need to consciously reassess the inbuilt cognitive structures that are causing us to feel anxious.

So far, we have spoken in rather simplistic terms: We might hold an unconscious belief that ambiguity = danger.

In real life, and in real (messy) brains, the story is often a lot more complicated than this. Many theorists prefer, in fact, to talk not about single thoughts, ideas, beliefs, or interpretations, but about **schema**.

A schema is not just one thought or idea, but:

- A pattern of thoughts that organizes ideas into categories.
- A framework that determines how those categories relate to one another.
- A mental model, or an inner map or representation of the world.

We typically acquire our schemas early in life, but also from our culture, our experiences as adults, and the media.

One important thing about our schema is that once they're acquired, they tend to stay put—even persisting despite counterevidence. When contradictions arise, most of us would sooner adjust the facts to fit the schema than the other way around!

Because a schema is a cognitive tool that we use to help us understand and make sense of the world, it influences *everything*:

- What we pay attention to
- How we make sense of our perceptions
- The meaning we ascribe to things
- How we feel
- The ongoing quality and content of our thoughts

Implicit associations can reveal something about the way our inner schema are organized.

An implicit association is simply an *automatic and unconscious link* that we make between two mental concepts. This link then influences our attitudes, feelings, thoughts, and behaviors in the world.

In research psychology, scientists are typically interested in the way implicit associations lead to bias and prejudice. You can even test your own unconscious associations by trying the Implicit Association Test (IAT) online (https://implicit.harvard.edu/).

You might outwardly assert the wrongness of ageism, for example, but your quick and automatic responses reveal that your unconscious schema actually links "old" with "incompetent" and "young" with "competent," for example.

Schema and the implicit associations they reveal are:

- Automatic
- Outside of conscious awareness
- Highly influential on our thoughts, feelings, and behaviors
- Not necessarily reflective of reality

What does all this have to do with anxiety and overthinking?

Our current schema and implicit associations might be creating and maintaining our anxiety.

Consider, for example, that you may have an implicit association between "flowers" and "love."

This mental link is not strictly accurate, but it's unlikely to cause you much trouble in life.

But what if you had an implicit association between "money" and "failure"?

Or "my body" and "guilt"?

Or "work" and "trap"?

These links and connections are *deeper than beliefs*, and well below your conscious awareness.

You may never say out loud, "work feels like a trap" but that's precisely the structure of your underlying schema.

Implicit associations act like buttons or levers—whenever you think or experience something to do with money, for example, you also *automatically and unconsciously* think "failure."

Whenever you're reminded of your body, you are also *automatically and unconsciously* triggered to feel guilty for lifestyle habits you know you should drop.

You press that button, or you pull that lever, and the same thing happens, every time.

If a link is connected in any way with threat, then naturally it will create or exacerbate feelings of anxiety.

Overthinkers tend to have links, associations, and schema that center around threat.

Here's the point at which we return to the most interesting aspect of implicit associations:

➜ They are NOT NECESSARILY REFLECTIVE OF REALITY.

If we can truly internalize changes to those schemas that create anxiety for us, then we do so much more than just lower anxiety—we change the entire shape of our perceptions, our feelings, and our thoughts.

It's the difference between rewriting a line or two or code vs. installing an entirely new operating system.

In an interesting study published in the *Journal of Consulting and Clinical Psychology,* the authors find that **although anxious schema can be stubborn, they can change**—and when they do, this change is strongly predictive of a reduction in anxiety symptoms (Teachman et. al., 2008).

By shifting the mental links we hold, we change the "gut-level meaning" associated with certain situations and so reduce our anxiety.

Our schema changes shape, the internal map of reality that we have shifts, and the story feels different.

We update our mental model.

And then we *feel* different.

➜   You might be wondering: How on earth can a person change their implicit associations if they're automatic and unconscious?

The good news is that *you don't have to.*

That might sound strange.

But consider what an implicit association really is: an *initial* reaction. In other words, it's the first thing you think. Your easy default.

But that's not the end of the story!

Because **what you do next also matters**—in fact it's often the *only* thing that matters.

- We may not be able to change our initial, pre-programmed, knee-jerk responses to certain triggers.
- We may not be able to easily shift associations we learned in childhood.
- We may not even be aware of all the ingrained links and assumptions we carry around with us.

But what we *can* always do is to stop, be mindful, and consciously choose our next move.

Your *initial* impulse doesn't have to be the last or only one.

You don't have to take everything you automatically think at face value, you don't have to take your deepest convictions seriously, and you don't have to continue on with an association just because it's the one you had first.

You can *think again.*

We cannot always see our unconscious schema, and we're not always fully aware of the associations and patterns we're operating from. But one way we can learn a little more about them is to **watch for "giveaways."**

A giveaway is a little "tell" that reveals something true about your unconscious schema. It's a quick and automatic behavior that discloses the real beliefs that influence your life—regardless of what you might officially say out loud or even convince yourself of.

Want to know about your unconscious schema?

- Then notice what you **do**—especially under pressure, or when there's not much time to think.
- Notice the thoughts, feelings, and assumptions that most readily pop into your mind.
- Notice what your "default" is—your most likely emotion, thought, and behavior at any point in time.

Anxious overthinkers can have all sorts of vast and complex mental schema, but they tend to have one thing in common: a kind of *doom thread* linking everything together.

A default perception of threat.

An overarching mood of fear, dread, or pessimism.

A deeply ingrained personal story of passivity or hopelessness.

It's as though the anxious mind is a tangled mess of millions of different threads, but almost every thread leads to the same node right in the middle—*THREAT*.

Pull on any of the threads, and you feel anxious.

Cutting those threads means reassessing our implicit associations and gradually reorganizing our mental schema. In the meantime, it also means being aware of the way our current schema work—and realizing that *just because we have certain associations doesn't mean we are destined to let them run our lives.*

At any time, regardless of our initial impulses, we can **consciously choose to act differently.**

Let's see exactly how that's done.

How to rebuild your mental scaffolding

We've already seen that implicit associations can be long-standing and deeply embedded. So, the first step:

- Don't beat yourself up for having these internal schema, links, and associations. Remind yourself that even if they're unhealthy or maladaptive, they *did* serve a purpose at one point. Be kind and don't judge yourself too harshly.
- Let go of any expectation that you will root out *all* your unconscious fears, biases, prejudices, and implicit associations. It's not about perfection. It's enough to simply be aware and to practice choosing to put your conscious, rational mind in charge.

Step 1: Be aware of and track "felt urgency"

Do you suddenly feel like things have gotten a whole lot more intense?

Does something feel really urgent, and really high stakes?

This could be a sign that an anxious schema has been activated in you, i.e., a thread has been pulled and that THREAT node deep in your unconscious mind has been tugged at.

What now??

Just pause and notice it happening.

➡ Ask yourself to put a name or label on this feeling or urge.
➡ Ask how urgent this impulse feels to you, on a scale of 1 to 10.

(PS: It can be a relief simply to acknowledge that *felt* urgency is not the same as urgency).

Example: You're suddenly convinced that you're really ill and in grave danger. The more you think about this weird new physical symptom you've noticed, the scarier it seems, and soon you can't stop thinking about it.

Label: "Anxious."

Impulse: "I just want to go online and Google to find some answers…"

You rate it as an 8 or 9—it all feels pretty life-or-death.

You tell yourself: "I'm feeling anxious. The impulse to research online *feels* urgent right now."

No arguing or engaging—just make a little space for the possibility that feelings of urgency or danger might not imply real urgency.

Step 2: Stay with the feeling

Implicit associations and habitual responses can't be *fought*—they can only be gently, gradually faded away over time. Starved out, if you like.

How?

Repeatedly give yourself evidence that the cognitive links you've made are not true or useful.

One way to do this is to just sit with your anxious feeling *without doing anything.*

- No rushing in to "fix" anything
- No anxiously looking around for an answer or a resolution
- No grasping for reassurance or explanations
- No storytelling or interpreting what it all means
- No judgement

Just sit and notice that feeling for a few moments.

Give yourself a moment—a lot can change in just 90 seconds!

Then ask, "How does this feeling rate now, on a scale of 1 to 10?

Remember, you're not arguing with yourself or trying to win a war. All you're doing is giving yourself enough time to ride out the initial urgent impulse and retrain your initial association.

Example: Perhaps after sitting with your anxiety for a moment, you notice that it goes down a few points. Not to zero, but it *does* fade. What does that tell you?

Step 3: Slow down and choose to act consciously

Even within a few minutes, the initial impulse and anxious association will have arisen… and possibly started to fade again.

- Notice the feelings coming…
- Notice them going again…
- Finally, notice the opportunity you now have to intentionally evaluate the options available to you, so you can act *on purpose*— rather than impulsively.

You've become aware of your *first* feeling. Now take the time to choose your *next*.

Often, there's nothing you need to do. Sometimes, though, you'll be faced with a decision to make. In that case,

- What are your values?
- What are your long-term goals?
- If you were the person you wanted to be, how would you act?

There is great freedom in realizing that you can be anxious, you can be uncomfortable, and you can be unsure—*and yet still act well.*

We can feel nervous and unsure and awkward and uneasy, and we can still make the kind of healthy decisions that help us live the lives we want to live.

Example: After the anxiety intensity peaks and fades a little, you remind yourself of all the good things in your life, and of all the things that matter to you. Then you consciously choose to step away from the internet for a while and instead move towards those good things.

Are you still nervous about that weird symptom? Yes, a little. But the important thing is that you're no longer being *controlled* by that feeling. You are controlling it.

Summary:

- Anxiety sensitivity means interpreting neutral inner sensations as dangerous, and it can create and exacerbate anxiety spirals. Breaking free isn't about stopping the sensation—it's about changing the interpretation.
- Break reactivity cycles by naming the loop you're in and finding an alternative "explanation." Then practice mini-tolerance to teach yourself that you can *stay with* sensations without fleeing, fixing, or judging.
- Anxiety worsens when you believe you are helpless and at its mercy. Instead, adopt a mindset where you focus on what you can control, and take action—even if it's only small.
- People who tend to interpret ambiguous situations as threatening are more likely to experience anxiety and panic. Rather than endlessly overthinking the "threat," we can reappraise the root cause: the interpretation that labelled this experience as a threat in the first place. Be OK with "I don't know."

- Cognitive change comes before symptom change. Before we can reduce anxiety, we need to consciously reassess the inbuilt cognitive structures that are causing us to feel anxious.
- Our schema may be deeply embedded, but *they can change.* Slow down, become aware, and reclaim your power to act consciously, despite the felt urgency.

Chapter Two – Building Tolerance

One of the biggest triggers for overthinking is uncertainty.

Rumination appears and poses itself as a solution: "Uncertainty feels bad. But if I overthink, I can figure it all out and feel better."

However, the opposite is actually true—we find peace and balance by *facing* uncertainty, not by chasing endless mental schemes designed to *eliminate* it.

Wellbeing is not the prize you finally earn when you've successfully removed all discomfort and adversity from your life; rather, **it's the ability to be strong and resilient right now, even with all your discomfort and adversities intact.**

In this chapter we'll investigate ways to gradually cultivate a non-anxious mindset:

- "I can tolerate uncertainty and be OK."
- "I can cope with discomfort."
- "I can survive other people's dislike, disappointment, or disapproval."

It is normal to feel stress and anxiety.

It is normal to feel discomfort.

It is normal for life to feel uncertain, unfinished, and imperfect.

Wellbeing means the ability to emotionally regulate through this stress—and not wait until it's gone before we allow ourselves to feel OK.

Train tolerance for "maybe"

"Uncertainty is an uncomfortable position. But certainty is an absurd one."

\-   *Voltaire*

Big idea: One common anxious metacognition is, "I must be certain." Uncertainty intolerance is at the root of much anxious overthinking, but we can always take steps to learn to accept and embrace uncertainty, rather than anxiously trying to eliminate it.

As the name suggests, **uncertainty intolerance is the lack of ability to accept ambiguity, incompleteness, or the unknown**. This "psychological allergy" is really a knot of related beliefs and assumptions about threat, control, and predictability.

It's not even the threat itself that is feels unbearable, but the cloud of "maybe" that surrounds it. It's no exaggeration to say that some people would prefer to know *for sure* about a negative future event than to be in the dark about something that only *might* turn out negatively.

The uncertainty itself is felt as a threat. Overthinking is a coping response:

- I must worry
- I must prepare
- I must find out more
- I must get reassurance
- I must analyze
- I must avoid or procrastinate

In short, one way or another, **I must be certain— and only then will I be OK.**

Uncertainty intolerance often looks like:

- Reassurance seeking
- Checking and re-checking
- Excessive planning
- Rumination
- Never-ending information seeking
- Difficulty making decisions
- "Analysis paralysis"
- A relentless need to be in control
- An insistence on sameness, predictable routine, and guarantees

It's unsurprising that uncertainty intolerance is strongly associated with anxiety, depression, OCD, autism, and difficulties with procrastination. In short, a person's attitude towards the unknown has far-reaching implications for *every* area of their lives.

The rule of uncertainty tolerance is a little something like:

→ **I cannot be safe/restful/OK/happy/functional unless I have perfect certainty.**

As a corollary to this rule, it then follows that my only path to being OK is to seek out certainty. I don't feel OK. That means I must keep on overthinking, planning, analyzing, and worrying until I DO.

Stepping outside of this belief takes effort.

Your mind will tell you that the way out of your discomfort is to keep mentally churning until you eventually uncover that little something that will give you the assurance you need.

But the problem was never that you lacked certainty.

The problem was the belief that you *needed* certainty to be happy.

The new belief we want to acquire:

→ **I don't need perfect certainty to be safe/restful/OK/happy/functional.**

Chasing reassurance, guarantees, control, and (the illusion of) certainty seldom makes us feel better anyway. Perfect guarantees are rare in life, and often, gaining a little additional reassurance or information doesn't actually last long, and we soon move on to needing more.

And more.

The way out is *not* to find certainty, but to learn to face and accept a degree of uncertainty.

A study published in the journal *Behavior Therapy* (Dugas et al., 2010) found a CBT program that focused on challenging the "I must be certain" belief lead to measurable improvements in the study participants' anxiety levels, and that it outperformed a program that focused on applied relaxation only.

The techniques that follow closely resemble the program they would have followed.

How to build your uncertainty tolerance

Does building uncertainty tolerance mean forcing yourself to like the unknown and get a kick out of ambiguity?

Fortunately, no.

We all have different tolerance levels for uncertainty, and a degree of apprehension in the face of the unknown is far from unusual.

When we speak of training greater tolerance for uncertainty, we are not saying that we are trying to make ourselves *like* the unknown. Rather, **we acknowledge that uncertainty is uncomfortable, but we can cope with that discomfort, and we needn't rush to eliminate it.**

We train ourselves with a new mindset: "I am uncertain. And that's OK."

Technique 1: Drill "good enough is enough" decisions

We are very often required to make decisions in the absence of perfect knowledge. When faced with that margin of uncertainty, the old rule might tell us, "Keep researching or analyzing until you feel more certain."

But that only means that you procrastinate making a choice, overanalyze things to death, or get overwhelmed with the options you have in front of you.

Gently shift out of this mindset by changing the rule.

- Instead of: "I can only act when I have complete knowledge."
- Change it to: "I can act when I have sufficient knowledge."

Basically, good enough is enough.

The irony is that if we postpone decisions for long enough, we may end up with something far worse than a less-than-perfect decision—we end up doing *nothing*.

Dr. Martin Luther King Jr. is thought to have said, "Take the first step in faith. You don't have to see the whole staircase, just take the first step."

We may delay action because we feel like we don't know enough information to make the right choice. But sometimes, the very act of taking the first step is precisely what brings more information into our world! We do something and instantly the situation shifts, we learn something, or we feel differently. In other words, it is *acting* that brings more certainty, not overthinking.

Remember: It's easy to believe that decisions are far more decisive and impactful than they are. In reality, most decisions in life are multi-step *processes*—we act, we observe the result, we adjust accordingly, then act again, and so on, adapting as we go.

Certainty comes gradually... but usually on the *other side* of action!

If we stay where we are and fail to act, the amount of information we have stays precisely the same. We ruminate ad ruminate, making guesses about an outcome that we would actually feel more certain about if only we acted.

➜ Ask yourself, "What is a **sufficient** amount of information that I need in order to make this particular decision, right now?"

For example, I'm in a restaurant and there are fifty different things I could possibly order. I'm panicking.

How do I choose the right thing?

The *best* thing?

I notice my anxiety and gently remind myself: I don't have to choose the best, most perfect thing. I only need to choose something that's good enough.

Because good enough is enough.

I very quickly make a short list of five things I am 80% confident I'll enjoy, then pick the first one that comes to mind, without overthinking it. When my mind jumps in with, "But what if there's something else that's better?" I counter with, "Well, there could be. But this is a good choice, and a good choice is good enough."

Technique 2: Have a daily "maybe" practice

It may sound strange, but you can cultivate tolerance for uncertainty simply by increasing your exposure to it. Prove to yourself that you actually *can* withstand not knowing, and that life goes on—sometimes very well—even in the absence of perfect knowledge.

- Deliberately choose to leave a small mystery unresolved or a question unanswered. Let a mildly uncomfortable feeling simply be, without trying to remedy it in any way:
  o Don't Google an answer to figure something out for sure.
  o Don't check or confirm something—just let it be.
  o Don't ask someone or seek out reassurance.
  o Don't dream up a backup plan or rehearse.

What you are doing is gently challenging the idea that you *need* this kind of control.

Technique 3: Uncertainty mindfulness practice

A very quick and easy way to push back against the "I must be certain" dogma is to simply be more mindful—and watch how certain urges, discomforts, and feelings rise and fall.

1. Notice when you're feeling anxious.
2. Give the sensation a label. "I'm finding uncertainty uncomfortable and threatening right now."
3. Rate this sensation's intensity on a scale of 1 to 10.
4. If you like, you can also rate the degree to which you believe the thought, "I must be certain" or "I cannot be uncertain and be OK."
5. *Then, pause. Just wait. Do nothing.* Don't reach for a behavior to lessen the intensity of that discomfort—and that includes internal behaviors, like reassuring yourself mentally.
6. In ten minutes or so, take another reading. What is the intensity of your discomfort now? Is your belief "I must be certain" still as strong?

Inevitably, your strong anxiety feelings do fade, even if they are very strong to begin with. What's more, you may notice that the intensity of your feelings can drop *even without certainty.*

This practice is about helping your brain learn that "maybe" is survivable. That the discomfort of something unknown is certainly unpleasant—but not dangerous.

Technique 4: Self-guided graded exposure

In its structure and function, fear of uncertainty is a lot like fear of spiders or heights or crowded spaces.

And just like those fears, we can teach ourselves to be more comfortable with uncertainty by gradually exposing ourselves to unknown situations while preventing escape.

→ In this case, "escape" means any behavior (including internal behaviors) that attempts to control, reduce, or eliminate the discomfort and fear.

Escape behaviors are what we do to feel safe. When we deliberately expose ourselves to feared situations *while preventing these safety behaviors*, we're teaching our minds that certainty isn't as necessary as we believe, and that facing uncertainty won't actually hurt us.

Here is the basic process:

- **Create a "bravery ladder"** of actions or situations that progressively increase in intensity. What matters is that each item is a little more anxiety-provoking than the one before it.
  - Example: You panic when travelling without a detailed and highly controlled itinerary. Your ladder may look like this:

i. Pick a hotel and go there without analyzing reviews ahead of time.
ii. Let somebody else pick the hotel.
iii. Go on a weekend trip and leave one day completely unplanned.
iv. Go on a weekend trip and leave both days unplanned.
v. Book a trip for the very next day.

- **Work your way up.** Start with the easiest, most manageable rung of the ladder. The goal here is not just to force yourself to do unpleasant things. The point is to train a new mindset. You achieve this by facing your fear (uncertainty) *without reverting to safety-seeking or escape behaviors.*
  - Example: Your first task is to go to a hotel without obsessively checking reviews first. As you avoid checking, you notice your anxiety increases. Stay there with it. Maybe notice all your anxious thoughts that object to the uncertainty. Tell yourself, "I am uncertain. It's uncomfortable, but I'm not in any danger."
- **Increase intensity.** When you can comfortably face the uncertainty on one rung of the ladder, without escape, then you can choose to move to the next rung. What you don't want to do is rush and force yourself—this may backfire and teach you that uncertainty really is dangerous. Instead, only move to the next rung once you're at least 80% able to manage the one below it. Take your time. Be kind to yourself.
- **Bank your gains.** After every move up the ladder, pause for a moment to acknowledge the distance you've travelled. Give yourself a chance to reappraise and reframe your beliefs. Let it sink in that you *can* do difficult and uncomfortable things.
  - Example: After going to a hotel without anxious research and planning ahead of time, you notice that you actually have a good

experience. In fact, after repeating the exercise a few times, a completely new thought starts to dawn on you—not knowing what kind of hotel experience you'll have is sometimes a little bit *fun*! You teach yourself that sometimes, not knowing can be exciting.

Over time, these techniques will train new beliefs, like "uncertainty isn't dangerous," and "good enough is enough." You learn that not only can you survive the discomfort of not knowing, but that repeated exposure can desensitize you to uncertainty, shifting your appraisal of it from "threat" to "opportunity."

Later, in chapter three, we'll take a look at more advanced ways to use exposure methods.

Build "I can handle it" confidence

"You have within you right now, everything you need to deal with whatever the world can throw at you."

\-   *Brian Tracy*

Big idea: Your brain's self-preservation mechanism habitually weighs two predictions against one another:

- **How bad is the outcome going to be?**
- **How well will I be able to cope with it?**

Anxious overthinkers tend to have highly catastrophic interpretations, paired with almost zero belief in their own competence.

Let's say you've just attended an important and nerve-wracking interview at the company of your dreams, for the job of your dreams. You prepared for days, you've done your very best, and… now you wait.

You've been told to expect a decision within a few days, but these few days prove to be *torture*. Not knowing feels like it's killing you!

And then you start to ruminate.

Your head feels a bit like a bowl of spaghetti, but when it comes down to it, there are just two main thoughts holding all this anxiety together:

- **It's going to be awful**
- **I won't survive it**

In fact, this particular combination of beliefs, in one way or another, plays a key role in almost *all* anxious thoughts loops, panic spirals, and overthinking traps.

We greatly overestimate the upcoming catastrophe, and we greatly underestimate our own ability to cope with it when it arrives. See if you can spot the combination:

- Public speaking: "I'm going to totally humiliate myself and I'll never recover."
- Social anxiety: "They're all going to hate me and I'll be alone forever."
- Phobias and fears: "I'll pass out in terror and I don't even know what I'll do then."

Many of us have experience with **catastrophic thinking**, imagining and elaborating on the worst-case scenario.

Many of us also have a **low sense of self-efficacy**, meaning we have little confidence in our ability to cope with life's trials and challenges.

However, there is something particularly anxiety-provoking about *both together.*

Imagine a seesaw.

On the one side: our prediction of how catastrophic and threatening an event will be.

On the other side: our prediction of how well we might cope and survive.

It's the balance between these two that determines how anxious we feel.

After all, consider that if I predict that an outcome is going to be very bad, but I also predict that I am very strong and able to manage that outcome, then I won't be anxious. The seesaw is balanced or even tipped in favor of "I can do it."

On the other hand, if I have predicted that I have basically zero ability to cope with *anything* that life throws at me, then even a small negative event will tip the seesaw in the wrong direction, and I will feel anxious.

So, how do we reduce anxiety?

- We reduce our catastrophic predictions
- We increase our coping predictions
- Or both!

In fact, this is exactly what Casey et. al. concluded in their 2005 paper published in the journal

Cognitive Therapy and Research. The researchers wanted to know if a CBT treatment program would help participants with panic disorders, and if so, *why*.

They found that:

> "Patients in the Standard CBT condition reported significantly greater shifts both **towards higher panic self-efficacy** and **lower catastrophic misinterpretation of bodily sensations** during treatment, as well as a significantly lower level of panic severity at posttreatment. Changes in catastrophic misinterpretation of bodily sensations and panic self-efficacy contributed significantly more to prediction of panic severity than did assignment to either Standard CBT or a Waitlist Condition."

In other words, what seems to make the biggest difference for people is whether they experience shifts in two key beliefs: self-efficacy and catastrophic interpretation. Interestingly, being able to make this shift was the thing that ultimately mattered—not whether a person did the CBT treatment program or not.

To put it another way, the mindset *least* associated with panic, anxiety, and rumination is this:

- **It's probably going to be OK**
- **And I can manage it**

Uncertainty and the anxiety seesaw

You'll probably have noticed that the quantities we are measuring on this "anxiety seesaw" are *predictions.*

This is important: They're not absolute fact or truth, but guesses, estimations, and perceptions.

Naturally, **the mind tends to make more predictions in the face of the unknown.** When you don't really have the facts or you don't really know the truth, then you guess. You make an estimate and appraise the situation as best as you can, given what you have.

However, some of us make *especially* inaccurate guesses in the absence of full knowledge.

➔ "I don't know what will happen, but it will probably be bad. And I don't know what I'll do, but I probably won't cope at all."
➔ "I haven't heard back from the company yet, so I guess that means they're not going to hire me and I'll never find a job as good as that again."

Uncertainty and the unknown can be major triggers for anxiety precisely because they prompt this kind of anxious guessing. Not only do we imagine the worst possible outcome we can think of, we also somehow forget all the resources and skills we have at our disposal to cope. Plus, we dismiss all the times we've coped with challenges just like this one in the past!

The way forward will naturally be to swing the seesaw the other way:

- Decrease catastrophic thinking
- Increase self-efficacy thinking

We are going to focus on the second one—increasing self-efficacy. There are a few reasons for this, but primarily, it's *easier*.

It can be difficult to lessen the intensity of catastrophic thinking that is already well underway. It may be relatively easier to turn attention away from the feared outcome entirely and focus on building more confidence in your own ability to cope, no matter what happens.

Let's see how to do just that.

How to build self-efficacy when it comes to uncertainty

Predictions are slippery things.

When you're making guesses and estimations, *anything* goes.

The only way to gently challenge any predictions you make—whether about a catastrophic outcome or about your own ability to cope—is to literally *compare your prediction with reality.*

In other words, **was your prediction right?**

The exercise below is a way to start gathering real counterevidence that pushes against the distorted predictions that are fueling anxiety. Two big caveats, however:

1. We need to pay honest attention to the truth of our predictions.
2. We need to give ourselves the opportunity to really *test* them.

Step 1: Keep a "predictions" log

Let's return to our earlier example.

→ "I haven't heard back from the company yet, so I guess that means they're not going to hire me and I'll never find a job as good as that again."

Let's break that down:

→ You predict that they won't hire you (catastrophic outcome).
→ You predict that you will never find a good job again (low self-efficacy).

Step 2: Check back in on your predictions

After a few days, come back to your log and compare your guesses with what has actually unfolded in reality.

Look at both predictions you made.

Was the outcome as catastrophic as you believed it would be?

Were you as helpless and hopeless in dealing with the outcome as you thought you would be?

If you had to rate your predictions according to their accuracy, what score would you give them? It may help to literally write it down!

Almost always, you'll find that your predictions were greatly distorted.

- I predicted __________.
- What actually happened was __________.
- This tells me that __________.

The great thing about this exercise is that *it doesn't actually matter what the outcome is!*

It's all data. Reality will either confirm your predictions or disconfirm them. Either way, you'll learn something.

- Maybe you predicted they wouldn't hire you, and they did. This is proof that *catastrophic predictions can be wrong.*
- Maybe they didn't hire you. You predicted that you wouldn't cope and that you'd never find a good job again. But a few weeks later, you did. It was difficult, but you managed. This is proof that *coping predictions can be wrong.*

Step 3: Keep returning to the facts

The next time you're in an anxious overthinking spiral, go back to your predictions log.

- Remind yourself that *catastrophic predictions can be wrong.*
- Remind yourself that *coping predictions can be wrong.*

After all, you'll be looking at actual proof.

At the time, you may well have believed those predictions 110%. *But they were still wrong.* They felt real and intense and urgent and true. And they were wrong.

And that means that the anxious predictions you're making *now* could also be wrong.

Once again, reassurance and forced positivity are not necessary here. We just need to gently tip the seesaw in the other direction.

To lower anxiety…

→   We don't need to say: "Nothing bad will ever happen to me and besides, I'm invincible!"
→   We just need to say: "Outcomes are usually not as bad as I fear, and I'm often stronger and more capable than I give myself credit for."

Ask yourself:

•   Will the outcome really be a *total catastrophe*? Or is it more likely that it will be fine, or at the very worst a little awkward or uncomfortable?
•   Is it really true that if something goes wrong you'll be completely, utterly unable to cope? That you won't be able to stand it, and will just curl up and die? Or is it more likely that it might be unpleasant, but you'll find a way to get through it?

Balancing the seesaw is about bringing both predictions back into the realm of ordinary plausibility.

The anxious mind is nervous about *not* making such predictions. "How else am I going to keep myself safe? And what if the worst-case scenario really *does* happen?!"

We need to be honest about the role that rumination plays for us. Anxiety might disguise itself as intelligent problem solving or useful "preparation," but there's an easy way to see through this disguise:

"Is this anxiety prompting me to take beneficial action?"

- Real problem solving focuses your awareness on an issue, prompts sensible action, and once a decision is made, that intensity diminishes.
- Fake problem-solving (i.e. anxious overthinking) never goes anywhere. It doesn't precipitate action. It just brings your attention to the problem, over and over again, amplifying itself over time.

The more entries you make in your predictions log, the more you'll prove to yourself—with hard evidence—that the things you most fear and dread never actually happen. You'll also prove to yourself that all that rumination and worry never *does* anything for you—and it's usually wasted effort.

When you feel anxiety hitting again, go through your predictions log, and consciously tell yourself:

- "Even though right now it feels like my anxious predictions will *definitely* happen, I have felt that way before, and I've been wrong."

- "I have been in challenging situations before, and I have coped."
- "I have character traits, skills, strengths, and tools to help me manage difficult situations. I am not on my own, and I can always seek help and information."
- **"Challenging things happen in life. But they're usually not as bad as I predict, and I know I can handle things, whatever happens."**

Reduce overthinking fueled by people-pleasing/reassurance cycles

"The courage to be happy also includes the courage to be disliked."

-       *Ichiro Kishimi and Fumitake Koga*

Big idea: Anxious overthinking can be maintained by certain interpersonal dynamics. These include seeking reassurance, people-pleasing, and conflict avoidance. It's not enough to re-appraise our own *thinking patterns*; we also need to consider the *social patterns* that make overthinking more likely for us.

In the previous section, we looked at the example of uncertainty feelings around planning a trip or holiday. We saw how certain safety-seeking behaviors can reinforce the belief that *"I must be certain."*agt

But what about when those behaviors involve other people?

It can be tricky to unpack our own habitual thought patterns.

It can take time and hard work to change our mental models and update our beliefs.

But we also need to be aware that those models and beliefs are plugged into the wider social world—a world that sometimes doesn't really *want* us to change!

An intriguing study published in the *Journal of Consulting and Clinical Psychology* gathered together some research participants who'd been diagnosed with GAD—generalized anxiety disorder. They assigned these participants to different groups:

- **Group 1** received applied relaxation and self-control desensitization.
- **Group 2** received cognitive therapy.
- **Group 3** received a mix of both.

The researchers followed up with all participants 2 years later, and *all of them* showed significant improvement in anxiety symptoms—most of them no longer even meeting the criteria for diagnosis (Borkovec et. al., 2002).

So, it would appear that doing something— *anything*—about anxiety is generally effective. But perhaps the most interesting part of the study was that "interpersonal difficulties remaining at posttherapy [...] in a subset of clients, were negatively associated with posttherapy and follow-up improvement."

➜ In other words, although all participants showed some improvement, **those with lingering interpersonal difficulties tended to show poorer improvement overall.**

 What might those "interpersonal difficulties" be?

We'll look at three major ones:

1. Reassurance-seeking
2. People-pleasing
3. Conflict avoidance

Even if you consistently do the work to reappraise your own unhealthy thought patterns, you may still get lured into anxious overthinking loops *by external social pressures and temptations.*

Consider the examples below—and note how much overlap there is:

Reassurance seeking (i.e., "outsourcing certainty"):

• Repeatedly asking someone, "Are you angry with me?" or "Do you love me?"
• Getting second (and third and fourth) opinions from health professionals or asking others to give you their opinion on your medical symptoms.

- "Checking by proxy." For example, asking again and again, "Are you sure you locked the door?"
- Repeatedly asking for feedback, or for teachers, colleagues, and bosses to confirm that you've done a good job and that things are OK.
- Taking pains to pre-empt offense in conversations, apologizing, checking that you haven't said something wrong, or repeatedly confirming that other people understand you and/or aren't angry or unhappy.

People-pleasing:

- Saying yes automatically to invitations, requests, or demands even though you don't want to. As a result, over-committing yourself and dreading letting the other person down.
- Directly or indirectly eliciting validation, praise, and reassurance from others that you have value in their eyes.
- Neglecting your own needs and downplaying your own personality so that you can prioritize other people's needs, expectations, opinions, and behaviors.

Conflict avoidance:

- Ignoring disrespectful behavior and boundary violations in an attempt to maintain harmony.

- Using passive aggression to meet needs in an indirect way, when the direct way may be too difficult or risky.
- Staying silent to avoid confrontation and disagreement—but then feeling resentment grow.
- Allowing others to disregard your boundaries and failing to assert dissatisfaction for fear of causing offense.

These behaviors may provide temporary relief in the moment, but they can set up cycles where anxiety only worsens over time.

We may have a range of anxiety-promoting beliefs:

- "I have to be certain."
- "Ambiguity is threatening."
- "It's going to be a catastrophe and I won't cope."
- "I'm not in control of my thoughts."

Embedded in the social world, these beliefs can look like:

- "Other people can or should help me be certain."
- "I have to please, accommodate, help, and prioritize other people to be safe."
- "It will be a disaster if someone disagrees with me or is disappointed in me. I won't survive their dislike of me."
- "I can't trust myself. I need others to confirm my perceptions."

What is at the root of all this reassurance-seeking, people-pleasing, and conflict avoidance?

That's easy: FEAR.

Each of these is a **fear-driven attempt to escape discomfort, ambiguity, and uncertainty—using other people as safety-seeking props.**

Each of them represents an unwillingness to *stay with* discomfort, ambiguity, and uncertainty.

Caveat: Human beings are social animals, and of course it's normal and healthy to want to be kind, maintain harmony, and collaborate. There is nothing wrong with seeking support, advice, or comfort. There's nothing wrong with being accommodating, compassionate, or helpful to others.

The only question is **why** we do it.

If we feel *compelled* to do all these things out of fear of what will happen if we don't, that suggests that these behaviors are playing a less-than-healthy role in our lives.

Authors Ichiro Kishimi and Fumitake Koga tell us that happiness requires **the courage to be disliked.**

Perhaps it also requires:

- **the courage to be uncertain,**
- **the courage to face ambiguity, and**
- **the courage to withstand discomfort.**

Proponents of Adlerian psychology, Kishimi and Koga suggest that interpersonal harmony actually means not interfering with others, nor allowing others to interfere with us.

If we can focus on our own path and hold onto our own self-determined value, then we no longer need to anxiously cling to the expectations, needs, opinions, demands, and perspectives of others.

- We learn to tolerate uncertainty within ourselves, so we don't need to ask others to supply it for us.
- We find purpose, self-worth, and meaning in our own lives, so we don't need others to tell us that we're OK.
- We know that we have an equal place in the world, and that we don't have to give it up in order to be with others.

The truth is that it's *this* courage that allows us to live free from anxiety.

People-pleasing, reassurance-seeking, and conflict avoidance only offer a temporary illusion of peace. In the long term, they actually undermine our ability to lead calm, grounded lives.

How to take control of interpersonal triggers

Technique 1: One-ask rule

Does your anxious safety-seeking take the shape of seeking reassurance?

That's OK. Give yourself permission to ask—but take control and tell yourself that you will ask once *and then stop.*

Take careful note of the reassurance you're given.

Tell yourself that the time for reassurance seeking is now over.

Then notice what happens.

Notice how your discomfort rises as you feel the urge to ask again. Watch that impulse come… and watch it go again. You may like to use a scale of 1 to 10 to monitor how that urge changes over time.

It may feel *really* urgent in the moment, but does it still feel that way ten minutes later? What about half an hour later?

Notice that it's possible for your anxiety to fall without resorting to safety-seeking behaviors.

- **TIP:** When the urge to ask for reassurance pops up, the trick is not to default to internal or hidden reassurance.
  - Don't say: "There there, it's OK, you're doing fine, everything's fine, there's nothing to worry about…" That's just more reassurance.
  - Instead, say: "This feels uncomfortable. I feel like I want to escape it. I don't like this feeling, but I can handle it."

Technique 2: Try a mini assertiveness practice

If you're prone to people-pleasing and conflict avoidance, this one's for you.

The irony is that *indirect* attempts to relieve anxiety often end up creating more anxiety for you in the long-term. It's often easier to face the momentary discomfort in a *direct* way.

For example:

- You fear saying no so you say yes—and then find yourself desperately overthinking how you're going to meet your commitments, and how you might disappoint people.
  - It would have been easier and simpler to just say no upfront, *even though it would have been temporarily uncomfortable.*
- You fear asserting your own preference or boundary so you keep quiet—and then find yourself stewing in resentment. You're soon angrily ruminating over how you're being taken for granted.
  - It would have been easier and simpler to speak honestly and assertively, *even though it would have been temporarily uncomfortable.*

This exercise is about giving yourself small opportunities to be uncomfortable in the *short-term* so you can prevent overthinking and rumination in the *long-term.*

People-pleasers often think they're taking the easier route through life, but the opposite is true—avoidance inevitably prolongs trouble and adds to the discomfort. Once you truly grasp the idea that *directness is actually the easy way out*, things start to change.

Try committing to one small assertive act a week:

- Voice disagreement or a different opinion ("I don't quite see it that way.")
- Make a minor request for something that would make your life easier ("Could you please confirm by Friday?")
- Gently assert a boundary ("Can't do weekends, I'm afraid.")
- Express a need or make a small request ("Can I please have the dressing served on the side?")

Remember: Your task here is not to somehow find a way to have your needs met without ever upsetting other people. It's not to find some magical way to be what everyone else wants you to be while still staying authentic and non-anxious.

Rather, the goal is to understand that sometimes there *will* be a little friction or discomfort—and that you can handle it!

➜ You don't have to force yourself to be perfect.
➜ You only have to find the courage to be as exactly as you are—discomfort included.

Has somebody responded with a little annoyance at your boundary?

Is someone slightly disappointed that you're not choosing to prioritize them?

Is someone continuing to be vague, confusing, or disagreeable?

That's OK!

It's your chance to practice being calm, grounded, and comfortable in yourself anyway.

"I can sit with this discomfort. I'm safe. I don't have to *do* anything to get away from this feeling. It will pass when it does. In the meantime, I can live a good life."

Shift the engine of overthinking: Cultivate real coping

"Do not pray for an easy life, pray for the strength to endure a difficult one."

\-   *Bruce Lee*

Big idea: Healthy, resilient people don't experience less stress—but they are more skilled at coping with that stress. Overthinking may be your current coping mechanism, but the good news is that it's always possible to try a new, easier strategy.

Everyone feels anxious from time to time.

For some of us, the experience of anxiety or any intense emotion feels a little like this:

- "I don't really know what's happening to me or why."
- "I don't like it and I don't want it."
- "The problem is *out there.*"
- "The solution to this problem is to *escape.*"

For others, the experience of anxiety and intense emotion feels different:

- "I can pause to identify and label my experience."
- "It's uncomfortable, but I accept it."
- "The problem is *in here*, with how I'm thinking about things."
- "The solution is to *approach* something better."

It's easy to assume that people without anxiety issues simply experience less anxiety. But it's probably more accurate to say that they experience all the same tensions and discomfort as anyone else—but **what differs is what they do next.**

Our schemas and beliefs around anxiety can make us feel that there is something especially wrong with us, or that our lives are uniquely stressful, unpleasant, or difficult. We might compare ourselves to others and think, "It's so much easier for them."

But let's look at things in a different way:

→ Being alive is intrinsically difficult. No matter who we are, life will eventually present us with setbacks, adversities, frustrating unknowns, moments of unfairness, disappointment, confusion, or fatigue.
→ Each of us uses different tools to help us manage all this.
→ The difficulty is universal. But the tools we use to cope vary significantly—and that's what makes all the difference.

Analogy: You live in a house and, like all houses, it gets dirty over time. Dust appears, the dishes need to be washed, the trash piles up.

However, you have a collection of tools to help you keep on top of things: laundry detergent, a vacuum cleaner, a sponge, etc. As a result, your house stays (mostly) clean.

Now, if all you had to clean your house with was water, old newspapers, and a broken bucket, you'd be in a completely different situation.

It's the same with stress, anxiety, and difficult emotions. This mental clutter and mess steadily accumulate in our psyches, but with the right tools, we stay on top of things and keep our internal space tidy, safe, and comfortable.

Without the right mental tools, we struggle. The old newspapers and the broken bucket work— kind of. But then we look at how much cleaner other people's houses are and think, "It's so much easier for them."

But the truth? *They've just got better cleaning tools.*

One of the very best psychological "tools" we have is **emotional regulation**. When we regulate our emotions, we learn to identify, accept, and manage our changing experiences in a healthy way.

We are less reactive and more intentional.

We are mindful, resilient, and make better decisions.

Our lives are not easier. *We are stronger.*

Emotion regulation therapy (EFT) = a treatment approach focused on helping you find and use the right tools to help with everyday distress and anxiety.

Important: We don't eliminate those emotions or get rid of them forever; we *regulate* them.

Emotional regulation is really a set of different skills, all of which we will be considering in this book:

- **Attention** – learning to be present and recognize what's actually going on with us.
- **Allowance** – learning to "sit with" experience rather than avoid and resist.
- **Distance** – learning to defuse from our experience.
- **Reframing** – learning to reappraise our interpretations and evaluations.
- **Responding** – learning to reflect, then make good decisions.

Overthinking is a coping mechanism, and it works… just not very well. Like the broken bucket!

The goal with EFT is to shift towards more effective coping mechanisms. We regulate ourselves when we become aware of what we feel, accept it, find a little psychological distance, and maybe change the story we're telling.

From *that* position, we can make a conscious decision to move towards something that matters to us, which will make a material difference in our lives.

A study in the *Journal of Consulting and Clinical Psychology* found that patients with GAD (generalized anxiety disorder) experienced significant improvements in their symptoms after receiving a treatment course of EFT (Mennin et. al., 2018).

They demonstrated:

- Less worry and rumination
- Better quality of life
- An enhanced ability to function in day-to-day life

What's more, around half of the participants also experienced depression, and their depressive symptoms also improved after the EFT treatment program. At follow-up the researchers found that the effects were still stable at nine months.

All this, the authors explain, comes down to a greater capacity for self-regulation. Though every participant had been diagnosed with GAD, they had now been given the right tools to cope.

How to turn your thought processes around

Typically, EFT is a treatment protocol employed by mental health professionals in more structured therapeutic contexts. Luckily, the very same tools and techniques are available for anyone to learn and apply in their own lives.

Before we take a look at some of these tools, however, we need to consider an important mindset shift that needs to happen first:

- **Overthinking is a tool—just not a very good one.** At first it may feel hard to give up your broken bucket, especially if you're not yet convinced about the alternatives. Remind yourself that you are replacing a less effective tool with a more effective one, that's all. In its own way, overthinking has worked for you in the past. That it doesn't work anymore doesn't mean you're doing something wrong—it means you're learning to do something better.
- **There are alternatives.** You could have all the tools in the world at your disposal, but if you don't truly believe that it's possible to change, or if you're not even aware that those tools are available, you're going to stick with the broken bucket. Stay open-minded. Experiment. Be flexible. Remind yourself that you don't *have to* keep doing things the way you have been doing them.
- **Coping takes patience and practice.** Abandon the thought, "The right thing will be easy and come automatically." Health and wellbeing are skills—not fixed traits. A healthy mind is the result of *consistent habit*, just like a clean home is the result of regular cleaning. It will take time to master the skills of emotional regulation. Time to learn to use the tools. And it's OK that it takes time! Be

patient with yourself and settle in for the long haul.

Tip 1: "Name the state, name the need"

Rather than being trapped inside an anxious experience, step outside of it, give it a name, and call it out for what it is.

"Hey, I recognize you."

It can be helpful to put words to the state that you're in—and remind yourself that you are indeed experiencing something temporary.

- "I'm in threat mode right now."
- "I'm in a shame state."
- "I'm running the uncertainty routine."

Once you've put a name on the state you're in, make sure not to condemn or judge yourself for it. Instead, ask:

"What is my mind trying to protect or get right now?"

- **Certainty?**
- **Approval?**
- **Safety?**
- **Control?**

You're not feeling the way you feel for no good reason. So, what's the reason? Cast curious, compassionate eyes on the function of the current condition you're in.

Not to judge, but to understand.

Example: You leave a social situation and notice yourself turning inward and ruminating. It's like your mind is speeding up and the thoughts are growing darker and more desperate... was everyone really annoyed with you? What did X mean and why did you have to say Y?

You immediately notice what's happening and put some distance between what's happening and yourself, *without* escaping or resisting. It feels really awful and terrifying, but you accept it. You speak kindly to yourself, saying, "I've been here before. That panicky, spirally sensation.... the queasy feeling that I'm losing control of my thoughts... this is me in overwhelm mode."

You ask, "What is my mind trying to protect or get?" You reflect. You realize that you found the social situation extremely complex and confusing, and now your brain is trying to help by overthinking it all. Why? It wants to help you find a degree of control again.

Overthinking is your current tool for meeting the need for control. But now you start to become curious if you can identify a better tool...

Naming the state, naming the need is the first step to switching to an alternative coping strategy.

If you look at a broken bucket and you're able to say, "This bucket is broken. It's an attempt to meet the need to carry water" then two things can happen:

- You can be honest about how well it meets that need.
- You can start to identify other tools that can better meet that need.

In our example, you can make the connection: "Overthinking is my brain's first attempt to help me feel in control. But I can feel safe and OK without overthinking. In fact, there are things I can do right now to regain a feeling of control and self-determination in my life."

Tip 2: The "two-motives map"

This technique will never take you longer than a few minutes to do, but the results are truly impactful.

On a piece of paper, draw two columns:

- Avoid
- Approach

In the *Avoid* column, list everything you're trying not to face or to feel.

In the *Approach* column, list everything that matters to you, your goals, and your real-world scope of action.

➜ Sometimes our coping strategies can center around avoidance, escape, resistance, and denial. Overthinking usually lives in the avoid column.

➜ Instead of becoming better at avoidance, challenge yourself to shift focus entirely, and look at all the things you can *move towards* right now.

➔ Remember you don't have to argue with whatever you write down in the Avoid column; it's just a matter of gently changing where you put your attention.

This takes enormous pressure off of yourself—you don't need to feel perfectly OK or have everything figured out in order to make your next step a good one.

> *Example*: Realizing that your overthinking is trying to help you regain control, you do the "two-motives" exercise and find yourself listing in the Approach column all the things you actually *do* have some control over.

Micro-approach step

The next step from here should be obvious; commit to one small action on the Approach side. You want to choose a behavior that goes against the drive and force of your current overthinking spiral. You want to choose an act that is not about escaping, but about choosing, approaching, and deciding.

This could be:

- Sending that email draft that you've been procrastinating.
- Do the first two minutes of a task you've been dreading.
- Take a five-minute walk outside to breathe and clear your head.

- Call up a friend and share how you feel or ask for a little support.
- Do something you love, help someone, or make something.
- Assert a tiny boundary, ask a direct question, or express an opinion.

The important part is that you can do all this even though your mind may still be chattering.

> *Example*: After your stressful social event, you may still be thinking, "What did X mean? Why did I have to say Y?" and so on, but you still make the conscious choice to do something that you know aligns with your goals and values. You go to the gym like you said you would. You focus on the workout in front of you, deriving satisfaction and a feeling of control from your disciplined effort, your hard work, and your good form. Eventually, the post-event rumination dies down a little, and you move on with life.

Afterwards, when you get home, you recognize what's happened.

> *"I was tempted to reach for my old overthinking strategy earlier today. Though I was anxious, I did not overthink and instead regulated my emotion by naming how I felt, and taking healthy action in a different direction. It was tricky, and I didn't completely eliminate my anxiety. But I feel stronger now. Next time, I'm going to practice more self-regulation instead of looping."*

Summary:

- Uncertainty intolerance is at the root of much anxious overthinking, but we can always take steps to learn to accept and embrace uncertainty, rather than anxiously trying to eliminate it. By gradually exposing yourself to uncertainty rather than avoiding it, you can build uncertainty tolerance.
- Drill "good enough is enough" decisions and learn to act even when you don't have perfect or complete knowledge. Have a daily "maybe practice" where you deliberately expose yourself to short moments of uncertainty.
- Your brain's self-preservation mechanism habitually weighs two predictions against one another: How bad is the outcome going to be? And how well will I be able to cope with it? Anxious overthinkers tend to have highly catastrophic interpretations, paired with almost zero belief in their own competence.
- You can reduce catastrophic thinking while increasing your sense of self-efficacy: "It's probably going to be OK, and I can handle it."
- Anxious overthinking can be maintained by certain interpersonal dynamics. Watch out for people-pleasing, conflict avoidance, and "outsourcing certainty"—i.e. using other people as safety-seeking props. Try the "one ask" rule or a weekly mini-assertiveness practice. Remember that interpersonal friction, disappointment, or having to assert boundaries doesn't mean you are unsafe.

- Healthy, resilient people don't experience less stress—but they are more skilled at coping with that stress. Anxiety is normal—what matters is what you do next. Overthinking may be your current coping mechanism, but the good news is that it's always possible to try a new, easier strategy.
- Emotional regulation is like daily "mental hygiene" that keeps your internal space clean. Name the state/mode you're in and identify what your mind is trying to protect or get. Then, find a different way—a new tool—to meet that need.

Chapter Three – What Healthy Thinking Looks Like

What does non-anxious, balanced, healthy, constructive, and empowered thinking actually look like?

If you're an overthinker, it's understandable that at times you wish you could just *switch your brain off.*

However, the remedy for overthinking is not *no* thinking—it's better thinking. And that means retraining an entirely different attitude towards your own mind, and what it's for.

In this chapter, we're looking at:

- How to cultivate a healthy and realistic relationship with your thoughts.
- How to anchor into more concrete, functional, and flexible thinking.
- How to break free of *avoidance*, and start facing your fears head-on.

Defuse from thoughts and do what matters anyway

"You don't need to eliminate your negative thoughts. Take them with you and do what matters. What a relief!"

\-   *Shamash Alidina*

Big idea: Sometimes we tell ourselves that we can only be happy once we get on top of our faulty thinking, once and for all. However, real liberation comes from knowing that we can experience anxiety, uncertainty, and discomfort, and still live a rich, meaningful life anyway—right now.

Overthinkers can be hard on themselves—*really* hard on themselves!

They can turn everything (including their own anxious rumination) into something to beat themselves up with.

They can feel like they're broken, crazy, irredeemable.

Without knowing it, they develop **the belief that anxiety is standing between them and the good life.** In other words, as long as they experience negative thought patterns, then they cannot live well, accept themselves, succeed, or be happy.

But what if this belief is part of the problem?

Action and Commitment Therapy (or ACT) is not about finding that magical solution to get rid of anxiety once and for all. Instead, it's about "living well anyway."

- You can be present.
- You can do what matters.
- You can live according to your values.
- You can have a meaningful and full life.
- *And you can do it even though you experience anxiety.*

How?

We do it not by changing our thoughts.

We do it by changing our *relationship* to our thoughts.

Thoughts are passing electrochemical events in our brains. They're words and symbols. That's all. They don't have the power to define who we are, and they don't control us.

Negative thoughts are normal.

The grounded attitude is: Don't fight thoughts, defuse from them.

Cognitive defusion is simple: It's when we create distance between us and our thoughts, and remind ourselves that thoughts are just that—thoughts.

Not commands.

Not absolute truths.

Not permanent realities about who we are.

When we are defused from thoughts, we stop over-identifying with them. We look at them more objectively. They do not control us; *we* consciously decide what we want to do with *them*.

And this is the big relief of ACT: **You don't have to control your thoughts. Instead, take control of what you do.**

Of how you live.

Of the kind of person you want to be.

Instead of believing that we have to reach some lofty standard of mental health, a state of enlightenment, or an unrealistic degree of control, we can shift our attention to living by our values and principles.

That means asking what matters to us more than anything, then acting in that direction.

Yes, you may feel anxious. Yes, all sorts of experiences and perceptions may enter and leave your conscious awareness. And through it all, you can still be there—constant in yourself, and present in the moment.

A study in the journal *Behaviour Change* found that ACT was at least as effective as CBT at reducing generalized anxiety symptoms—and that in many cases it might work more quickly than CBT (Avdagic et. al., 2014). The authors concluded that the reason both CBT and ACT work is because they both support *psychological flexibility.*

Psychological flexibility is not really a single skill but an attitude encompassing a range of skills:

- The ability to be **present** (not always trying to escape or avoid discomfort).
- The ability to stay **open** to experiences (not getting trapped in rigid thought patterns).
- The ability to adjust behavior so that it aligns with **values**—even when emotions are running high (not fusing with thoughts or being reactive).

From the ACT point of view, the goal of a healthy human life is not to find a way to permanently run away from pain. Instead, it's to actively cultivate a state of mind where we can be open, present, and values-driven—whether pain is there or not.

How to build more psychological flexibility

The good news is that psychological flexibility is something we can learn. It doesn't matter where you start from or how easy or difficult you find it at first, because every experience is grist for the mill.

No matter what is going on for you right now, you can pause, become aware, accept where you are, and choose to take just one tiny step towards the things that you believe in deep down.

The next time you feel an overthinking storm coming on, consider running through the following three steps:

1. Bring accepting awareness to the moment you're in.

2.   Defuse and stay open to other possibilities.
3.   Commit to one small values-driven action.

Step 1: Awareness and acceptance

Many of us feel a kneejerk resistance to the suggestion that we accept our bad feelings.

It's important to understand, though, what we are doing when we accept the reality in which we find ourselves:

- We are not saying we approve of what is happening.
- We are not forcing ourselves to pretend we like it.
- We are not claiming to be responsible or saying that we chose this experience.
- We are not giving up on the possibility of changing for the better.
- We are not saying we deserve how we feel or that want to continue feeling that way.

All we are saying is that the reality we are in right now is... the reality we are in right now.

No resistance, but no clinging either.

Acceptance simply means acknowledging reality for what it is, without attaching to it, judging it, clinging to it, or telling convoluted stories about what it means.

- **Non-acceptance:** "I'm anxious and that's a problem. There's something wrong and it needs to be put right. This isn't fair. I judge myself for feeling this way. I wrestle with it and want it to go away. I feel bad that I feel bad. I'm going to analyze it. I'm going to tell myself what I think should happen..."

- **Acceptance:** "I'm anxious. OK."

Overthinkers can mistake acceptance for *resolution*.

We think we can only accept a situation once we've internally processed it somehow, made it better, made it make sense.

But we can accept ambiguity and the unknown. We can accept a situation that is confusing and unfinished and unresolved. We can even accept our own impatience, overwhelm or confusion.

"I think this acceptance idea is BS and I don't like it."

➔ You can even learn to accept *that*!

Part of psychological flexibility means having the courage to be present with your experience right now, exactly as it is, without escaping or going into avoidance.

Analogy: Anxious overthinking is like a tug-of-war between you and your experience. You resist, you pull, you struggle against it. Acceptance is dropping the rope and choosing not to take part in that struggle anymore. It's not an effort in the opposite direction—it's the end of effort.

Step 2: Defusion and openness

Try to gain a little psychological distance with a defusion phrase, for example:

- "I'm having the thought that ___________."
- "Right now, there is _(insert emotion)_."
- "I am noticing that ___________."
- "I've started telling the old story I always tell myself when I'm stressed."
- "That's a judgment/guess/prediction/distortion."

Consciously reframe your anxious experience as a discrete mental event.

Not a command.

Not a permanent reality.

Not something that defines you as a person forever.

You can make that mental shift using language alone, but there are other ways to defuse from both your thoughts and your feelings.

- **Write the thought or feeling down.** See it there, in black and white, outside of your mind. Notice that you can move those words closer or further away from you. You can put them right in front of your eyes so that they're all you can see... or you can set them off to the side so that you can focus on something else. You can scrunch it up and throw it away, fold it up until it's small, or even burn it! You get the idea.

- **Use visualization.** Imagine that your mind is the clear blue sky, and emerging perceptions, emotions, and thoughts are just weather passing over that sky. Temporary. Always changing. And underneath it all, you are still that blue, depthless sky. You can use other imagery: A thought can be a balloon, say, floating higher and higher into the sky until it's the size of a pinprick. Another possibility is to see a thought as a bus stopping at a bus stop. Do you want to "board" this bus and have it take you to its destination? Or can you see that bus come... and then watch it go again without getting on?
- **Don't take yourself too seriously.** Repeat your thoughts out loud, but in a comical, jokey voice. Sing those beliefs and assumptions out loud in a silly way. Give your anxious thought patterns a name and character and make that character ridiculous. ACT therapists sometimes give the analogy of a bus filled with unruly and argumentative passengers. As the bus driver, you can be aware of their antics, but at the end of the day, you're the one who decides where the bus goes.

Step 3: Take a step toward your values

Your mind is anxiously chattering about something?

OK. Fine. Let it do that.

In the meantime, why don't you go off and do something meaningful?

This is the spirit of committed, values-driven action—and it's naturally a big part of "action and commitment" therapy.

Remind yourself, *"I don't need mental quiet to live my day."*

The irony is that you often *do* find mental quiet by letting go of the struggle and getting on with living your life.

Anxious overthinking is a rat race. It's a game that doesn't go anywhere, and there is no way to win. It's a game where the more you try to fight, the more you get tangled up.

So, stop trying.

Drop the rope and go and find something that truly fulfils you.

Switch your thinking style from abstract → concrete

"The most dangerous thing about an academic education is that it enables my tendency to over-intellectualize stuff, to get lost in abstract thinking instead of simply paying attention to what's going on in front of me. Instead of paying attention to what's going on inside me."

\-   *David Foster Wallace*

Big idea: Anxious overthinking is not just about the volume of your thoughts; it's also about the

style and *character* of those thoughts. **Maladaptive thought patterns tend to be abstract, overly general, and judgmental. But style can be changed!**

There's one unacknowledged reason why many of us are reluctant to let go of the overthinking habit: Deep down we believe that over-intellectualization is actually useful.

The interior life of the mind is a major part of many overthinker's identities.

They may be capable of a high degree of reason, creativity, and insight.

They may be intelligent and value intelligence.

They may be sensitive, deep thinkers.

And they may also use intellectualization as a *defense mechanism*—a way to avoid distressing emotions or to delay taking difficult action in the real world.

The mind is a phenomenal thing. Abstract thinking defines our species, and has been at the foundation of almost every human advancement. Language, philosophy, mathematics, art… all impossible without the ability to conceptualize, theorize, and imagine.

But overthinkers tend to be *over-users of this gift of abstraction.*

It may come as a surprise that overly abstract thinking is associated with depression, anxiety, and a general lack of wellbeing (Watkins, 2008, *"Constructive and Unconstructive Repetitive Thought"*).

In a paper investigating the effectiveness of an online CBT-program on rumination, the authors are careful to note that,

> "A maladaptive style is characterized by **abstract, overgeneralized, and evaluative processing,** whereas an adaptive style is characterized by concrete, specific, and contextualized processing (Mak et. al., 2024)."

So what exactly does this thinking style look like?

The abstract processing style is characterized by:

- WHY questions
- High-level conceptualization
- Overgeneralization
- Evaluation and judgment

For example, you may notice that you're feeling anxious and that you're suddenly aware of your heartbeat.

Your thoughts look a little something like this:

> *"Why is my life always like this? Why does this happen to me and nobody else? I have so much on my mind and now I have to worry that I have heart disease as well. Who designed humans anyway? What is the point of all this suffering? God must be having a laugh at my expense."*

Now, take a good look at the quality and character of this stream of thought.

- Notice the **why** question, and also notice that these are the kinds of questions that don't quite have an answer (or if they do, the answer will be an almost unfathomable can of worms!).
- Notice how these thoughts are **generalized**—they're about everything, about life, about God, about human nature. Not just what is happening right now (the awareness of a heartbeat) but the big questions of why existence must be this way, and what it could all possibly mean.
- Notice the **evaluation** and judgment implied—the experience is not just picked apart and analyzed, but condemned.
- Notice, finally, the utter impotence of this line of thinking. It may sound harsh, but these almost academic musings just... don't go anywhere. They don't terminate. They pose questions that are impossible to answer and open up avenues of thought that can theoretically go on forever.

It's not hard to see why this style of thinking leads to and maintains depression and anxiety! It amplifies the analytical powers of the mind but fails to *channel* all that power into any single useful direction.

Now, let's compare it to the concrete thinking style:

- HOW questions (as well as WHO, WHEN, WHERE and WHAT)
- Awareness of real, tangible facts
- Focus on specific details
- Contextualized thinking

Again, you notice that you're feeling anxious and you're aware of your heartbeat.

Here is your thought process.

"What's happening to me? I think I can feel my heartbeat. How is that possible? I haven't been exercising or anything. It is a little warm in this room so maybe that's it. Or maybe I just stood up too quickly..."

It's not just the content that is different here. This is a very different *style* of thinking:

- Notice the **what** and **how** questions. Notice how these questions are smaller, more targeted, and less abstract—meaning they can actually be answered.
- Notice how these questions keep awareness focused on the **specific** details of this moment—the sensation of the heartbeat, and how it may connect to immediate physical experience (i.e., it's **contextual**).
- Notice that there is **no evaluation** here. Just specific facts, in context, in a particular moment.
- Finally, notice that this kind of thinking has a direction. It has movement and a natural end point. It poses questions that prompt

genuine information-finding and problem-solving.

As you can guess, this style of thinking is associated with:

- Better decision-making
- Lower emotional reactivity
- Quicker recovery after stress or adversity
- Greater resilience

Rather than using our minds to endlessly elaborate on the *problem*, we can instead focus on possible *solutions*. If our thinking is neutral and not critical, we don't feel as overwhelmed. And by asking more concrete, grounded, and practical questions, we keep our minds tethered to reality—rather than encouraging it to spiral out endlessly.

While it is possible to be a concrete overthinker (more common in OCD, for example), the presence of overly abstract thinking is almost always a predictor of more anxiety, whereas concrete thinking styles tend to serve a protective function.

Does this mean that abstract thinking is bad or unhealthy?

Absolutely not!

Being able to conceptualize at a high-level is extremely useful and can help us see outside of and beyond our immediate experience.

But unless we're mindful, **it's exactly this ability to "go beyond" that can eventually lead to overthinking, catastrophizing, and anxiety.**

We need to learn to *choose* the mode of thinking according to our own ends, and what we're trying to achieve.

Now, before you make the fatal mistake of overthinking your overthinking, and over-abstracting your tendency to over-abstract, ask a few clarifying questions:

- Is my current style of thinking endlessly *opening up* anxious new possibilities, or is it helping me *narrow down* to a useful practical solution?
- Is my thinking leading me towards reasonable, values-driven action, or is it a "goes nowhere" train of thinking?
- Am I asking questions that don't actually have answers? Am I disguising doom-statements as questions?
- Am I genuinely moving forward, or am I looping and covering the same ground over and over again?
- Is my thinking helping me *avoid* painful emotions, or face them? Is my thinking helping me to *process* my situation, or *dwell* on it?

How to come back down to earth

Chronic overthinkers can sometimes find it very difficult to change gear and come into the concrete realm. If we believe that overthinking is useful and helps us to stay safe, we're obviously going to be hesitant to let go of it.

But with a little practice, you may find that there is extraordinary **relief** in dialing things down a notch and coming back to earth, as it were.

Overwhelm drops.

The sense of urgency and enormity lessens.

Everything shrinks down to a more manageable size.

That shadow of doom doesn't seem so heavy anymore.

Step 1: Catch and stop the "why spiral"

You'll know that you're caught in anxious over-abstraction if you're torturing yourself with endless why questions—especially the kind that only trigger more questions of the same character.

Learn to see *why* as gasoline on the fire of anxiety. These questions pose as earnest inquiries looking for resolution, but they often contain their own distortions.

Consider this question: "Why is life harder for me than it is for other people?"

It may trigger a long, long stream of overthinking that is completely irrelevant because—you guessed it—it's not really true that life is harder for you than other people. Don't "throw good questions after bad" and don't engage an unanswerable question by asking it more questions!

- Why me? (Would knowing the answer to this make the pain disappear?)
- Why is this happening? (A question with an infinite number of answers.)
- Why am I such an idiot? (A question, or a prompt to self-hate?)
- Why didn't he reply to my text? (In the most deeply philosophical sense, *who knows?*)

Questions without real answers are simply torture devices. They invite a kind of angst that will certainly make you feel bad but will do nothing to materially change your circumstances.

So, catch the spiral and then tell yourself: *"I'm caught in abstraction right now."*

See the mental spinning and churning for what it is.

It's not intelligent.

It's not a way to solve problems.

It's just being *stuck.*

Label that stuck feeling for what it is.

Step 2: Convert to a what, when, or how question

Abstracting thought is *expansive.*

Counter that with questions that narrow things down a little for you:

- What's the issue in one sentence?

o   What's one next step?

o   When exactly will I do it?

o   How do I start in the first 60 seconds?

The trick is to keep bringing yourself back to the real world, and the best way to do this is with *action*.

Instead of:

"Why do I feel so bad?" → "What can I do right now to feel a little better?"

"Why did I say that?" → "How can I apologize and make amends?"

"Why am I so messed up?" → "How can I take values-based action today?"

Sometimes, the best way to convert a question is to simply eliminate it. If there isn't any values-based action you can take, then you can safely conclude that this thought is just noise and can be disregarded.

"How can I turn my attention to something more worthwhile right now?"

Then try to focus on that.

Step 3: Make things smaller and more neutral

Notice when you're getting carried away with over-abstraction, and check:

- Are you making sweeping generalizations?
- Are you piling on judgment?

If so, try to make things *smaller* and more *neutral*.

- Are you worried about "life," or just the half-hour event that's happening this evening?
- Are you a complete and total failure, or are you just disappointed with your performance on one specific task, in one instance?
- Is your situation truly bad and hopeless, or is it just not quite what you wanted?

Make things smaller.

Be specific.

Remove value judgments—or at least tell yourself that you'll withhold judgment for a time.

Instantly, anxiety and overwhelm reduce.

Your mind can take anything and blow it up to gargantuan proportions, then announce to itself that everything's a disaster.

But you don't have to let it.

Instead, like David Foster Wallace says, just pay attention to what's in front of you. That's almost always way more manageable!

Use written exposure to break the avoidance loop

"Pain in this life is not avoidable, but the pain we create avoiding pain is avoidable."

\-   *R.D. Laing*

Big idea: Overthinking is a kind of avoidance. We think *around* a feared idea rather than face

it head on, so the fear always has a hold on us. The technique of "written exposure" allows us to build tolerance and teaches us that we can face fear and still function.

The concept of exposure therapy is not new.

The core idea is that **fear is kept in place by avoidance.**

Avoidance feels like a solution in the moment, but it only keeps us firmly in the clutches of fear, by reinforcing that avoidance:

Fear → avoidance → "I feel safe now" → "the fear must have been justified" → more avoidance

When we instead *approach* what we fear and expose ourselves to it, we break the cycle and teach ourselves that the thing we fear is not dangerous after all.

Fear → approach → "I feel afraid" → nothing happens → nothing happens → "maybe the fear isn't really justified" → approach further

Avoidance shrinks your world. Approach expands it.

To be effective, however, exposure needs to be **gradual** and **progressive**.

What we are exposing ourselves to is not even the feared object. We are exposing ourselves to repeated instances where the feared object does *not* produce the disaster that we predict it will.

We *don't* die.

It's *not* the end of the world.

We can experience discomfort and then... well, then nothing. That discomfort comes and goes, and then we move on with life.

While this "nothing happens," we watch as our panic and anxiety slowly falls. It's this that we are exposing ourselves to when we practice exposure therapy—this moment of **counterevidence**.

Usually, a hierarchy of fears is created, and we work our way from the easiest to the most challenging task or situation to the most intense one. For example, to gradually expose ourselves to our fear of talking to strangers, we could create an exposure hierarchy that looks like this:

1. Smile at the cashier at the supermarket
2. Greet the cashier
3. Strike up a very small conversation with the cashier
4. Smile at a random person on the street
5. Greet a person on the street
6. Ask a person on the street for the time
7. Strike up a conversation with a person on the street...

IMPORTANT: We need to *actually experience the fear, without resorting to safety seeking behaviors.* **We need to stay with the fear** long enough to learn that it isn't dangerous after all.

If you escape before you learn this lesson?

Then all you do is teach yourself another lesson— that the feared thing was dangerous after all, and what's more, your safety-seeking mechanisms are necessary and helpful.

Although with exposure therapy you may surely become "desensitized" over time, the goal is more about **creating a learning opportunity for yourself—one in which you can learn a new attitude towards the thing you fear.**

Exposure therapy is the perfect method for quickly overcoming specific phobias for things like spiders or heights. It's also great for training ourselves to be more comfortable in certain situations, like talking to strangers, as above.

But what about when your fears are a little more… abstract?

What about if you are deathly afraid of airplane turbulence or having an operation?

What if you have more complex, intangible fears like getting old or being abandoned?

These things are trickier to work into the classic exposure model… or are they?

- **In vivo exposure** = "in life" exposure—being in the physical presence of the feared object or situation.
- **Imaginal exposure** = *imagining* the presence of the feared object or situation and exposing yourself in that way.

Written exposure therapy (WET) is a kind of imaginal exposure. Based on the work of psychologist James Pennebaker, a pioneer of therapeutic writing, WET was originally designed for PTSD sufferers (Sloan & Marx, 2012; Sloan & Marx, 2025), but has since been used to address fears, phobias, and anxieties of all kinds.

So, how is it done?

WET writing is not just journalling or noting down your feelings. It is:

- Personal
- Free form
- Emotionally expressive

Most importantly, it's **concrete**—it's about the sensory details of exactly what happens next in the feared story. Through the written word, **you recall in vivid detail every aspect of the feared object.** You continue exposing yourself to that object in your imagination until the fear is extinguished.

"But isn't that the same as overthinking? I already spend all my time imagining my feared object in vivid detail!"

Here's the thing: *you probably don't.*

Anxious overthinking usually lacks detail. It also lacks movement and direction.

Your brain convinces you that something awful will happen, and you react emotionally to that thought, but you're never specific about what that might actually look like. What's more, the story doesn't really *go* anywhere. You pause the disaster film at the same scary scene and linger there.

The feared object terrifies you, but you can't bear to fully look at it. You don't dare look under the bed to see what kind of monster is there—if any. As a result, The Big Bad Thing becomes a vague, black shadow in your mind... and that disaster movie never quite plays out to the end.

The big surprise with imaginal exposure is that the "vivid detail" picture is often *less* frightening than our vague overthinking version!

Why?

Because it's more concrete.

Abstraction can elaborate on fears to infinity, but concrete things have known proportions. They are limited.

Plus, once you've already encountered something (even if only in your imagination), it instantly has less power over you. You've already faced it. In a way, the bad thing has already happened.

- "What terrible thing might happen?" → An open-ended question, the answer to which is likely to become more and more terrifying.
- "*This* specific terrible thing might happen, and how might I cope with that?" → Much, much less distressing.

Imaginal exposure asks you to replace vague, *avoidant* overthinking ("this is bad this is bad this is bad, oh my god this is bad") with thought that *approaches* a specific fear ("what *is* this?").

A study in the journal *Behavior Modification* (Goldman et. Al., 2007) found evidence that participants undergoing a written exposure program showed a reduction in their worry symptoms. Interestingly, the factor they identified as most predictive of improvement was an increase in uncertainty tolerance. **It's as though imaginal exposure to a feared object prompted initial anxiety... but also reduced the feeling of uncertainty.**

Once you understand the principles of imaginal exposure, specifically written exposure, then you don't need to enroll in a research program—you can try it out for yourself.

Before we explore how to do that, there's one important caveat we must consider:

DON'T LET EXPOSURE BECOME RUMINATION.

The moment you go into "why" and "what if," you switch from exposure into abstract analysis and overthinking.

Written exposure does not mean dwelling on stories, interpretations, predictions, or judgment. It means focusing on **specific, concrete sensory details** of the feared object.

It's not a disaster if you catch your focus drifting. In fact, it can be good practice to carefully discern the line between concrete and abstract. Just become aware of the style of your thinking, and gently shift it.

You're exposing yourself concretely to a feared outcome—not dreaming up fresh horrors or getting lost in investigation.

How to make your worst nightmare *boring*

Remind yourself that your worst fears, the ones you can barely stand to acknowledge, have a hold on you precisely *because* you can't properly face them.

It may seem far-fetched, but exposure is powerful enough to turn your attitude from sheer terror to "meh."

The process is simple, but the correct technique matters a lot.

Step 1: Pick ONE repeating worry theme

Yes, your fears and anxieties are likely all be tangled up together, but for ease and simplicity it's better to pick just *one* major concern, not a dozen of them.

It might be a worry about your relationship, anxiety around money or your work, a nagging health concern, or vague stresses around your performance, worth, or likeability.

Step 2: Identify the "worst-case story" for this worry theme

Inside your head, your anxious thoughts may *feel* infinite, and infinitely complex. But in reality, there's often just one main story that is playing out on loop.

Let's say that your worry is that your loving partner will wake up one day and realize what a loser you are, and leave. There's no evidence that this will happen, but you think about it all the time anyway.

This worry is painful and preoccupying, but quite light on the details. There may be vague fears and concerns:

- "What if they secretly don't love me?"
- "What if this relationship is just a ticking time bomb?"
- "What if they're preparing to leave right now and I don't even know it?"
- "Maybe they never loved me in the first place."
- Etc. etc.

Step 2 is to try to condense all of these painful thought "snapshots" into a single "worst-case story."

Keep it simple, and stick to the single story that holds all of the above together:

"I worry that I'm going to be suddenly abandoned."

The anxious mind tends to stop at the disaster, as though life simply doesn't go on after the feared outcome. But it's a good idea to "play the disaster film forward" a little and consider the things that happen next, too.

"I worry that I'm going to be suddenly abandoned, and then I'll be alone and sad. I'll be embarrassed that my relationship failed, and will feel worthless. I'll never find love again and my life will feel like it's over."

Step 3: Practice written exposure

Now, practice exposing yourself to this story:

- 3 to 5 sessions a week
- 15 minutes per session

Take care, because written exposure is not the same as ordinary journalling.

- Write in *first person* ("I am now sitting in my living room, all on my own").
- Write in *present tense* ("I tell people that I'm divorced now").
- Focus on *concrete* details ("Their side of the bed is empty now. The house is quieter. I feel heavy and tearful.")

Note: Here, "concrete details" also includes how you feel. Just be careful to imagine the emotion alone, without any judgment or interpretation. "I feel sad" is an emotion. "I feel like everyone thinks I'm a failure" is actually a thought in disguise.

Try to *avoid*:

- Problem solving (e.g. ruminating on how you'll quickly start dating again).
- Reassurance ("I feel tearful… but I know that I'm strong and I'll be OK").

- Avoidance (You find yourself writing about something else entirely, or making a nice-sounding theory about this break-up experience. Maybe you'll write a book! It could become a Netflix series…).
- Intellectualization, interpretation, and analysis ("I realize I have low self-esteem and it's because of my mother." "Maybe my ex was there to teach me something important about myself." "This is just typical of modern life/the human condition/men/women").

Remember that imaginal exposure is meant to replace in vivo exposure, so it needs to resemble as closely as possible the actual situation you're afraid of. It can help to think of it as virtual reality. It's less *literary novel* and more *action movie*.

Catch yourself getting overly abstract? Ask, "What does this look like as a concrete detail in my picture?"

Keep writing, without thinking about it too much, and stop after 15 minutes. There's no need to go back and re-read anything.

Step 4: After writing, do a 3-minute "re-entry" step

Done properly, written exposure *will* feel quite confronting.

Feeling pretty comfortable and at ease? It may be a sign that there is still some avoidance or intellectualization. Finding the task easy may also suggest that you have not yet fully identified the core of your fear.

➜ 15 minutes is plenty—don't force yourself to do more than this.
➜ 3-5 sessions is also adequate—take a break before attempting more.

After each session, debrief and take a moment to come back to reality and remind your body and mind that you are safe.

- Anchor in the sensory present again by identifying five things you can see, four things you can hear, three things you can smell, etc.
- Do a small, everyday activity that has zero emotional component, like a household chore or a basic grooming task.
- Go for a short walk, take a sip of water, have a snack, move your body, or cuddle a pet.

You might like to end your written exposure session by verbally affirming the progress you're making.

"I'm learning that I can face my fear and still function."

When you've completed around 5 sessions, pause to reflect and see what's changed for you. How does your response to the feared object at the beginning compare to now?

Summary:

- Sometimes we tell ourselves that we can only be happy once we get on top of our faulty thinking, once and for all. However, real liberation comes from knowing that we can experience anxiety, uncertainty, and discomfort, and still live a rich, meaningful life anyway—right now.
- We don't need to change our thoughts, but simply change our relationship to our thoughts. Negative thoughts are normal. Don't fight them, and don't fuse with them.
- Anxious overthinking is not just about the volume of your thoughts; it's also about the *style* and *character* of those thoughts. Maladaptive thought patterns tend to be abstract, overly general, and judgmental. But style can be changed! Try to switch to concrete, constructive, and present-based action to calm overthinking.
- Replace WHY with WHAT and HOW. Get specific. Drop the evaluation. Remember that we can *choose* the mode of thinking according to our own ends, and what we're trying to achieve.
- Overthinking is a kind of avoidance. We think *around* a feared idea rather than face it head on, so the fear always has a hold on us. The technique of "written exposure" allows us to build tolerance and teaches us that we can face fear and still function.
- Whether in vivo or imaginal, exposure needs to be gradual and progressive to work, and we need to prevent escape—even internally. Staying with the fear provides

counterevidence for our beliefs and extinguishes our fear over time. Keep exposure brief, targeted, and focused on concrete sensory details. Notice avoidant thinking and attempts to escape, and gently bring yourself back to the fear, until it no longer prompts as strong a reaction in you.

Chapter Four – Reorganizing Your Patterns

We've seen the attitudes and habits that characterize the overthinking mind.

We've also explored some of the attributes that define healthy, grounded, and peaceful thinking.

Now, we're ready to go a little deeper and see exactly how we can start making lasting changes to our own thought processes. In this chapter, we'll explore **the core principles of CBT—** including the common pitfalls that overthinkers risk falling into when they attempt to DIY the process!

We'll then zoom all the way out and investigate what is arguably the most important self-regulation skill: the ability to work on the **metacognitive level.**

This way, we **target maladaptive thought patterns at the root**, addressing multiple surface symptoms at the same time.

CBT skills for overthinking

"You have the power to change your thoughts and your thoughts have the power to change your life."

\-   *Ron Willingham*

Big idea: Cognitive Behavioral Therapy (CBT) is considered the treatment gold standard for many mental health disorders, including anxiety. Self-guided CBT is most effective, however, when it focuses not only on replacing distorted thought patterns, but making *behavioral changes* that align with those new beliefs.

Since its inception in the 1960s and 1970s, CBT has remained a staple treatment protocol for almost every mental health condition (Borkovec & Costello, 1993; Curtiss et. al., 2021; Bhattacharya et. al., 2022).

Following the early work of Albert Ellis, pioneering psychologist Dr. Aaron T. Beck had an insight that would forever change the face of talking therapy:

There is a **connection between thoughts, feelings, and behaviors.**

He reasoned that since all three are interconnected, if we change one, we cannot help but change the others. If we change our thoughts, we change how we feel, and consequently how we act.

Rather than endlessly analyze the past, Beck encouraged his patients to:

1. **Identify** negative, repetitive, or automatic thought patterns.
2. Gently **challenge** and replace them.
3. Make healthy **behavioral changes** in line with these new thoughts.

When it comes to overthinking, the CBT approach is to rework and replace unhelpful thoughts patterns so that the mind learns to stop replaying the past, catastrophizing the future, or dwelling in abstract hypotheticals.

But it doesn't stop there.

Unfortunately, today CBT is most commonly associated with "changing your thoughts." While **thoughts** certainly are a part of it, that's not the whole picture. Overthinkers in particular need to remember the other two components: **feelings** and **behaviors**.

- Focusing on changing thoughts alone → risks triggering more overthinking.
- Focusing on changing thoughts *and allowing them to inspire behavioral and emotional changes* → success!

We learn to identify distortions and biases in our own thinking not merely as an academic exercise. We don't change our beliefs and then just sit and wait for life to catch up. Rather, we change our beliefs and then **take deliberate steps to let those new beliefs ripple out through the rest of our lives—namely how we *feel* and how we *behave*.**

For those of us who are prone to overthinking, we can keep the CBT process from becoming yet one more exercise in rumination by staying:

- Practical
- Goal-oriented
- Engaged

It is not enough to merely "change our thoughts." We need to simultaneously acquire new skills, expose ourselves to our fears, and learn to emotionally regulate. Otherwise, all our "cognitive restructuring" will remain purely theoretical (that is, useless).

How to identify—and replace—your distortions

Before you jump in and start analyzing, it's worth getting familiar with the most common cognitive distortions. The thoughts and beliefs that tend to cause us the most trouble are the ones that are:

- Not true or accurate
- Not helpful
- Not kind

Shifting our most distorted beliefs and thoughts will yield the greatest results for us. But we need to know what to look for:

- **All-or-nothing, black-and-white, or polarized thinking**
  - "It's not perfect, so it's garbage."
  - Look for absolute language—*all*, *nothing*, *never*, *everyone*.
- **Mind reading**
  - "Everyone underestimates me."
  - Look for what is really a guess about someone's thoughts or feelings.
- **Generalization or overextrapolation**
  - "I failed at this, so I'll fail at everything I ever try."
  - Watch for sweeping statements that are all encompassing.
- **"Should" statements**
  - "I shouldn't be finding it this hard."
  - Also be alert for "must" and "have to."
- **Emotional reasoning**
  - "I feel guilty, so I must *be* guilty."
  - Look for the hidden assumption that your feelings perfectly reflect reality.
- **Catastrophizing (with a bit of "fortune telling")**
  - "It'll be terrible, I just know it will."
  - Look for unwarranted certainty about a negative outcome.
- **Mental filtering, minimizing, or exaggerating**
  - "I got good feedback, but it's just because they feel sorry for me."

- o   Notice the selective focus on only some details of a situation, while you ignore others. Also notice exaggerating the negative while downplaying the positive.

While there are many other cognitive distortions, the above are most common in anxious overthinking—and likely responsible for the bulk of those millions of distressing thoughts swirling around your head!

REMEMBER: While it can be useful to consider the truth, usefulness, or kindness of individual thoughts, it's usually more effective to identify distortions—they will point to larger negative thoughts patterns.

Let's take a closer look.

Step 1: Keep an overthinking thought record

For a week or two, try keeping a structured record of your thoughts.

Of course, you may feel like you have millions of thoughts a day, and it can be difficult to untangle a thought from a feeling from a belief from a perception from an interpretation...

Luckily, you don't have to get overwhelmed by any of that.

What you're mostly looking for is *cognitive distortions.*

Thinking is neutral.

But overthinking tends to be *distorted*—where there's distortion, there's likely overthinking, too.

Notice whenever you feel a rise in emotional intensity. Notice when that overthinking loop is starting up again. Then go to your dedicated "thought record" and quickly jot down:

- The date
- Your anxiety level, on a scale of 1 to 10
- Your current thought, in just a sentence or two
- The distortion you've identified
- One possible alternative

For example:

- Date: 12 Dec 2026
- Anxiety: 8/10
- Thought: "Life is impossible. Everything is just such a grind all the time."
- Distortion: This is overgeneralization.
- Alternative: "This current project is really uninspiring. I'm having trouble finding a way to get through these tasks."

Now, just note this alternative thought in your thought record for now. You don't have to rush to force yourself to believe in anything; your first job is just to get good at noticing distortions and making a little room for something else to be true.

Step 2: "Try on" the alternative

Step 1 doesn't need to be prolonged. After around a week or two, you will probably start to notice some repetition—the same thoughts and the same distortions appear again and again, just in different forms.

The goal is not to merely make a nice diary or stay trapped forever in analysis, however. The next step is to gently start adopting new, healthier, and more balanced thoughts.

This will take time!

The easiest way to do it is to notice when a particularly distorted thought appears, then remind yourself of the alternative you've already identified. Drill this mentally by repeating it to yourself again and again. Consult your thought record if necessary to remind yourself.

Here is where you begin to include the **feelings** element of the CBT trio.

After you've drilled the alternative, again check in on how you feel, and where your anxiety levels are.

- "Life is impossible. Life is a grind." → This makes me feel overwhelmed, resentful, scared, trapped and powerless. My anxiety feels like 8/10 when I think this."
- "This project is uninspiring. I'm having trouble with this task." → This doesn't feel great, but it's way more manageable. I don't feel trapped or resentful, just a little annoyed. It makes me feel like it's a problem that can be solved. Anxiety only 2/10."

Note that we are never required to fool ourselves, be unrealistically positive, or ignore the truth. All we need to do is *remove the distortion* so that we can have a clearer, more grounded, and more useful thought.

Step 3: Take action

The final component of the CBT trio is *behavior*.

Changes in thought patterns are purely hypothetical until they come alive in the actual arena of our lives—as behaviors, actions, and choices.

- You've identified the cognitive distortion.
- You've tried on a gentler, more reasonable alternative, and explored how it felt.
- The final step is to *make these shifts real* by taking action.

Behavioral changes don't have to be drastic to make a difference.

They just need to be one small step in the direction of your new thought or belief.

In our example, the thought, "Life is impossible. Everything is just such a grind," actually terminates the possibility of action.

It paralyzes you.

If it were true, what would be the point of acting?

But our new thought is more moderate: It's not "life" that is a problem, just this particular project. And it's not even the whole project, but a few tasks in particular.

If we focus on this more moderate appraisal, and we feel a lot less overwhelmed, then the next step is to ask, "What can I *do* now?" Inspired by our new alternative way of thinking, we can start making plans to act:

- Ask for help with these particular tasks
- Get support and guidance on how to do the challenging tasks
- Take a break to breathe and recoup
- Try to delegate these tasks
- Think of ways to avoid these kinds of tasks in the future

IMPORTANT: These small action steps are not just to get us out of our current predicament. What they're really doing is *restructuring our entire thought process.*

We are not passive, hopeless, and at the mercy of an "impossible" world. We are active agents working within manageable constraints, to achieve something we have faith that we can feasibly achieve.

This is not problem-solving—it's making deep changes to the way we think, feel, and behave.

And it's making changes to how these three interconnect.

Stop worrying about worry

"It's not what you do, it's the way that you do it."

-     *Melvin "Sy" Oliver and Trummy Young*

Big idea: Metacognition is the ability to think about the way you're thinking. By focusing not on the content of our overthinking, but on our beliefs about overthinking itself, we can make high-level changes.

Research psychologist and theorist Adrian Wells is credited with the creation of the theory of metacognition, and metacognitive therapy (MCT). This therapeutic approach is about HOW you think—not WHAT you think.

Or to put it another way, "it's not what you think, it's the *way* that you think it"!

Historically, CBT methods have tended to focus on the thoughts themselves. You are taught to look carefully at a thought and re-appraise it. Is it really true? What might be a better alternative?

CBT → Targets beliefs about the world.

MCT is a little different. Instead of grappling at the level of individual thoughts, you zoom all the way out and look at the *process* and *function* of those thoughts.

You notice your cognitive style.

You notice how you're thinking.

You notice not the individual thoughts, but the broader patterns and processes that precipitate those thoughts.

MCT → Targets beliefs about thoughts and thinking.

According to Wells and other MCT practitioners, change happens when we consider:

- How our attention works and where it goes.
- How we respond to our own thoughts, and the relationship we have to our own thinking.
- Whether our style of thinking is helping or hurting us.

MCT is especially useful for problems like overthinking, and it's easy to see why.

An overthinker's head may be full of ten billion rushing and looping thoughts.

The problem is not really whether each of these thoughts is "right" or "wrong"—the problem is that there are ten billion of them!

In other words, the rumination issue usually plays out at the meta-level—i.e. in *how* a person is thinking. Getting further tangled in the content of those thoughts may sometimes feel like a solution... but it's only more overthinking.

Be aware:

- "Changing your thoughts" can easily become *overthinking*.
- "Reflecting" can easily become *dwelling*.
- "Awareness" can easily become *obsession* or *hyper fixation*.

CBT is arguably the most thoroughly researched treatment modality and there is substantial evidence for its effectiveness. But us overthinkers need to be cautious, especially if we're going the self-help route. Without a real-life therapist to guide us, we could quickly drift from appraising the truth of different thoughts to just… ruminating again.

According to Wells, the goal of MCT is to address what he calls "cognitive attentional syndrome"—which is basically the cluster of patterns and beliefs that underlie worry, rumination, and over-sensitive threat detection.

Again, this is a characteristic *way* of thinking, not a collection of specific thoughts.

So, what do these metacognitive beliefs actually look like?

Recall that metacognitive beliefs are beliefs about thoughts and thinking.

There are broadly two types:

- **Positive** (for example, "worry is a way for me to stay safe")
- **Negative** (for example, "overthinking is ruining my life")

IMPORTANT: Both positive and negative metacognitions can be unhelpful.

CBT teaches us that:

- Thoughts are just thoughts.

- Thoughts are not necessarily facts.
- We don't have to respond to or engage with every thought.

The same is true for metacognitive thoughts. When we think, for example, "it's impossible to control my thoughts," that is also just a thought, not a fact.

You don't have to agree with this thought.

You don't have to take it as absolute truth.

You don't even have to pay attention to it at all!

Moving out from the *content* level and into the *metacognitive* level is often a powerful way to start shifting the long-held thought patterns that are keeping you feeling stuck.

➔ In CBT, you might work to change individual thoughts. But with MCT, you are changing your whole *relationship to* those thoughts.
➔ In CBT, you might consider the truth and usefulness of certain beliefs. But with MCT, you are looking more closely at *the role that worry itself is playing in your life.*

MCT can seem a little vague and abstract—until you put it into practice in your own life, that is. The evidence is encouraging. Wells et. al. (2010) has shown that MCT is better at managing anxiety than applied relaxation, and a recent study (Capobianco & Nordahl, 2023) shows that MCT's positive effects may exceed those of traditional CBT.

So, how can we practice a little metacognitive self-therapy?

How to retrain your metacognitive beliefs about overthinking

Without knowing it, **each of us has a set of "worry rules" that we allow to govern our mental life.**

These rules tend to be invisible to us—we don't acknowledge that they're there; we just follow them as though they were 100% true.

Example: The vet has just diagnosed your beloved pet dog with a health condition. They fully explain the most likely outcomes, instruct you carefully about the best course of treatment going forward, and tell you with some confidence that your dog will *most likely* recover within a month or two.

But you go home and worry about it.

You "research." You find yourself going down rabbit holes online. You play extended "what if" mental games with yourself. Your brain simply *cannot* leave this topic alone, and it keeps circling around the condition and its possible outcomes over and over and over again…

Thoughts:

- What if the vet is wrong and this condition is more serious than they think?
- What if the dog has been misdiagnosed entirely?
- What if the dog dies *tonight*, and I didn't do anything to prevent it?

Engaging with these thoughts—even if it's to argue against them or debate their veracity, is unlikely to make you feel better.

Why?

Because doing so leaves the big worry rules intact.

Worry rules:

- If I think a thought, there must be something in it (or I wouldn't be thinking it, right?).
- "Research" is actually a way I can stay in control and feel better.
- If I'm unsure about something, I'm not allowed to rest until I've resolved it.

These worry rules are metacognitions—beliefs about thoughts themselves. Notice that the above rules could apply not just to a sick dog, but anything. And notice that it's these that are keeping you trapped in rumination.

To really pull yourself out of the grip of overthinking, it's often better to work ON your worry rules, rather than WITHIN them. You need to target that second set of thoughts, not the first.

MCT proposes a few practical ways to give our unconscious worry rules a demotion:

- **Be mindful.** Detach from thoughts and look at them, rather than **through** them.
- **Challenge the rules.** For example, is it really true that if a thought pops into your mind, you *have to* engage with it immediately?

- **Take charge of your attention**. This means deciding whether a thought gets center place in your consciousness, or whether you choose to set it aside.
- **Change your relationship with your thoughts**. The thoughts are there. But you can choose how to respond to them, how seriously you take them, and what weight you'll give them in your life.

Step 1: Pay attention to your own worry rules

It can take a little practice to get used to thinking on the meta-level.

You need to stay alert and be mindful of the deeper worry rules underneath your own thought processes. One clever way to uncover these unconscious rules is to ask yourself what might happen if you were forcefully prevented from ruminating. Just notice: *What explanation jumps into your mind to justify overthinking?*

If that feels tricky, consider some rather common metacognitions, and see if any of them resonate:

- "Overthinking helps me perform and stay on top of things."
- "If I didn't worry, everything would fall to pieces."
- "If I keep thinking about this, eventually I'll find the solution."
- "Analyzing mistakes will save me from making them again."

- "Rumination is how I make sure I'm prepared, and that keeps me safe."
- "The more I understand, the more I can protect myself and avoid pain."
- "If I'm overthinking, there's nothing I can do to stop myself. My mind is uncontrollable."
- "My thoughts are dangerous."
- "Overthinking means I'm smart and switched on. It makes me a responsible person."
- "Unless I keep a tight check on myself, I'll go crazy or do something terrible."
- "I doubt my own sanity, and I don't trust my memory."

If possible, write these rules out for yourself. See if you can gain a little psychological distance from them (i.e., defuse).

Can you look at these rules neutrally, without engaging, but also without suppressing them?

Can you just observe them at a distance and see them as something you *think*, not something you *are*?

Tip: Don't beat yourself up as you practice these mindset shifts. Worry rules are just mental entities that stop existing when you stop thinking them. They're not actually harmful; it's just that using them brings you little benefit.

Step 2: Be honest about the effect these rules have on you

Our worry rules will *feel* like they are helping us. Like they are solutions, safety nets, or essential parts of our personalities that we simply cannot get rid of.

But this too is a metacognition! ("It's impossible for me to change the way I think").

Instead, make room for the possibility that these worry rules themselves are not helping, but are actually keeping you stuck in your distress.

Step 3: Challenge the rules

Once you are more mindful of the metacognitive rules you're living under, experiment a little to see what happens when you *don't* follow them.

Below are a few common and very effective ways to start challenging a range of common worry rules.

- **Worry postponement.** For many overthinkers, one rule is that if a worry pops up, we simply *have to* pay attention to it right this instant. You can gently challenge this by deliberately scheduling worry for later. Give yourself a fixed "worry window" every day for a limited time, for example ten minutes. When a worry pops up, note it down in a journal and tell yourself that you will attend to it, but later, on your terms, in your chosen worry window. Then put your attention elsewhere. "Thank you, brain, but I'm not focusing on this now."
  - Teach yourself that your unconscious worry rule isn't actually true—you *can* postpone

worries, and you don't have to respond instantly to every thought that crops up.

- **Attention training.** Another common rule is the idea that our minds are not really our own, and that our attention goes where it wants to, and we are merely passive passengers along for the ride. Challenge this worry rule by deliberately training your attention to go where *you* want it to go. We'll explore mindfulness in a chapter 5, but for now, practice focused awareness by simply setting a timer for 2 minutes and focusing your attention on a single object of your choosing. When your mind wanders, gently pull it back. Gradually, increase the time.
  - Teach yourself that you don't have to follow a thought just because it popped up. Your attention can be flexible and deliberate. You can detach and refocus at will.

The best thing you can do for rumination and overthinking is to *prove* to yourself unequivocally that it brings no real benefits to your life.

Our worry rules can convince us that overthinking serves a valuable purpose, and that without it life will be so much more dangerous, unmanageable, and confusing. But once you start gently challenging these beliefs, you give yourself the opportunity to try out alternatives:

- "I can choose whether or not to engage with my thoughts."
- "Worrying is not an automatic process, it's voluntary."

- "I don't need to control my thoughts to stay safe."
- "I can be prepared without worrying."

Reduce the behaviors that keep your anxiety engine running

"Scared is what you're feeling. Brave is what you're doing."

- *Emma Donoghue*

Big idea: The "transdiagnostic" approach is about looking beyond specific symptoms and investigating the underlying *processes* and *mechanisms* that are common to *all* mental health disorders. This way, we can use a single Unified Protocol to address a wide range of symptoms at once.

The DSM (Diagnostic and Statistical Manual) today contains definitions of *more than 450* distinct mental health disorders.

Under the anxiety umbrella alone we have generalized anxiety disorder, selective mutism, social anxiety disorder, PTSD, health anxiety, OCD panic disorder (with or without agoraphobia), and a range of specific phobias (with more than 500 distinct fears officially named, under five subcategories)...

Despite all this, **there is enormous diagnostic overlap**, not just between different anxiety disorders, but between other conditions like mood disorders, substance use disorders, or even personality disorders.

In psychology, the transdiagnostic approach shifts away from the specific outward expressions and manifestations of poor mental health, and towards the deeper underlying mechanisms that feed those specific symptoms.

Analogy: Psychological distress is a tree with countless branches, stems, and leaves. But all that variation stems from just a few important roots underground.

What are those roots? Not symptoms, but *processes*:

- Emotional dysregulation
- Repetitive negative thinking
- Uncertainty tolerance
- Avoidance behaviors
- Cognitive distortions
- Unhelpful metacognitions

What matters is not static symptoms and traits, but **functional processes**—all the mechanisms that are currently working to keep you stuck where you are.

- Conventional approach: "What symptoms do you have? What disorder can we diagnose you with? How can we treat that disorder?"
- Transdiagnostic approach: "What symptoms do you have? **What processes are currently maintaining those symptoms?**"

We've already considered many approaches that target mental distress at this level, including ACT (action and commitment therapy), MCT (metacognitive therapy), and CBT (cognitive behavioral therapy).

The so-called "Unified Protocol" is another treatment approach designed to address mental distress at the root, so to speak. There's encouraging evidence that this perspective can be as helpful or *more* helpful than "single-disorder protocols," i.e., those that focus on just one diagnosis (Farchione et. al., 2012; Barlow et. al., 2017).

How to run your own Unified Protocol

Transdiagnostic thinking takes a little while to get used to. It's not exactly a *what* but a *how*.

By shifting our perspective, changing our focus, and adjusting the way we talk about our own distress, we open up new possibilities for recovery and growth.

Instead of: "I have anxiety."

We shift to: "I habitually engage in behaviors that maintain my anxiety."

Instead of: "I'm an overthinker."

We shift to: "Overthinking is playing a particular role in my life right now."

Instead of: "I hate socializing because I'm an introvert."

We shift to: "My current thoughts patterns and beliefs are creating a tendency to withdraw socially."

Big difference, right?

The UP approach is not explicitly about healing, changing who you are, or fusing with a diagnostic label as part of your identity. Instead, it's about:

- **Active**
- **Practical**
- **Skill-building**

That means that it's not about who you **are** or the symptoms you **have**, but about what you **do**.

Sometimes, ironically, diagnosing and analyzing our own mental health conditions becomes a prime target for overthinking. It all gets very meta, and the mechanism loops and loops: "If I can just figure this all out, then I'll finally feel better, then I can rest and know that I'm safe and OK."

Unfortunately, "figure this all out" can sometimes mean endless introspective talk therapy, endless reading of psychology books, blogs, and forums, and endless self-scrutiny.

Instead, a transdiagnostic approach means we stay grounded and practical: We identify the behaviors that are keeping our anxiety alive, and work on those.

Below is a very simplified method for doing precisely that.

Spot your "overthinking safety behaviors"

Remember that overthinking is not irrational—it's something your brain is doing for a reason, and to a certain extent, it works.

It's just that, as we've seen, it doesn't work for very long, and it often comes with side effects that are at least as bad or worse than the original problem!

➜ List out the behaviors that you currently engage in to help you feel certain, safe, approved of, or in control.

For example:

* Re-reading messages and emails before sending
* Planning and rehearsing conversations
* Mentally reviewing or going over certain events
* Checking and re-checking
* Asking others for reassurance
* Googling, information-gathering, and online "research"
* Avoidance, denial, and procrastination
* Using certain props and shields, like a water bottle, a certain outfit, or your phone
* Overthinking, worry, and rumination

Importantly, behaviors can be *internal* and entirely invisible. As is common in OCD, for example, your safety behavior may be purely cognitive, and involve running through a series of ritualized thoughts, counting, reviewing, or planning.

It may be weird to think of overthinking as a behavior, but that's precisely what it is—a cognitive behavior designed to keep you safe.

At first, you may identify only one or two of these behaviors to put on your list, but with patience and awareness you may uncover more.

Choose one to drop by 10% today

You don't have *eliminate* these behaviors... just *reduce* them.

Example: Instead of re-reading your email or message ten times, agree with yourself that you'll do it just *nine* times.

- Pay attention to your anxiety levels
- Notice the oncoming urge to re-read
- Notice yourself choosing to lean on that safety seeking behavior just a little less
- Notice how you feel afterwards—was it as difficult as you thought it would be?

Over time, you can gradually reduce these behaviors in your life further and further.

It can feel really intimidating to have to make drastic overnight changes. After all, why would you want to drop behaviors that are there specifically to make you feel better?

Instead, go slow:

→ Don't put too much pressure on yourself.
→ Remember that your overthinking serves a purpose and meets a need.

→ Look for healthier ways to meet that need—such as a better tool, or values-driven action.

In the spirit of the transdiagnostic approach, don't worry too much about your specific symptoms—instead *keep focusing on what you're doing right now to maintain those symptoms, and what you can do instead that gently points you in the other direction.*

Example: You re-read the email nine times, and then instead of re-reading it a tenth time, you turn to a set of affirmations and statements you've prepared beforehand. You repeat these to yourself a few times:

- "I don't have to be perfect to feel safe."
- "Good enough is enough."
- "My performance doesn't define my worth."

Then you send the email.

Do the "opposite move"

It sounds overly simplistic, but it works.

Remember that anxious overthinking is often *avoidant*. By escaping into your mental world, your attention collapses in on itself and you are no longer engaging with the world—but rather with your own ideas, beliefs, and stories about the world.

In other words, you become *unmoored*.

Disconnected from the concrete reality around you, which would otherwise provide a kind of grounding.

With nothing "real" to anchor your thinking, it spirals out into ridiculous proportions. And because there's nothing to correct the path you're on, nothing to push against your distortions and assumptions, and nothing to provide any balance or perspective, you simply go further and further into the spiral…

➜ **One** way out is to simply *push against* this anxious momentum.

Instead of thinking, ACT.

Instead of escaping, APPROACH.

Instead of turning inward and introspecting, turn OUTWARD.

1. **Notice** your urge
2. **Call** it out for what it is
3. **Consciously** choose to do one tiny action in the opposite direction.

Note: it really only has to be a tiny action to halt the trajectory and start turning it around. You don't have to suddenly work miracles—just gently take your foot off the accelerator pedal.

Example:

1. I notice the urge to Google a concerning symptom.

2. I label it: This is a safety seeking behavior! And I know that even though it doesn't feel like it right now, it's actually maintaining my anxiety in the long run.
3. I still feel the urge. But I choose to go outside for a walk, without my phone, so I won't be able to go online at all.

Try not to get hung up on what the "opposite move" means exactly. The anxiety-reducing move doesn't even have to relate to the urge or impulse you feel; it just needs to pull you in the other direction.

Be active.

Approach.

Turn attention outwards.

Maybe you get up and move your body to "change the scenery"—and interrupt anxiety's grip on you for just a moment.

Maybe you choose to do one tiny, completely spontaneous action, just to break the inertia of "I must think about this" and loosen its hold on you.

Maybe you turn your attention onto something completely different—the sights, sounds, and smells of the world around you, or someone else's world. Ask a question, listen to the answer, and become engrossed in *their* mental world for a while!

Emotion allowance script

As you gently and gradually chip away at the behaviors that are keeping your anxiety intact, remember to talk kindly and constructively to yourself.

Think of the way an adult guides and instructs a child as they learn to do something new. Imagine a kind but helpful voice that explains what you need to do and how. This voice doesn't condemn you or frighten you—it's only there to help you develop and learn.

"OK, let's pause for a moment. What's happening here? Go slow. What have you learned about defusing? Try and remember some coping affirmations you wrote down earlier."

"Your mind is trying to tell you right now that you need to overthink, because that's the only way you'll neutralize all these bad feelings. Your mind is really smart, and it's always trying to help. You can have compassion for yourself while recognizing that this strategy of overthinking isn't working, though. Can you practice letting the feeling be here while you continue living? You don't have to be perfect. But you can take that first step."

"That's great, you're doing it now. It's getting easier and easier for you to notice and label overthinking when it happens."

"It feels a little better now that the peak has passed. What did you do a few moments ago that made things feel manageable? You can do that again."

This kind of self-talk may feel a little cheesy, but it's effective—you are teaching yourself how to use new psychological tools, and you're cultivating new behaviors.

You are slowly dismantling the engine that powers your anxiety and replacing it with something better.

Summary:

- Cognitive Behavioral Therapy (CBT) is considered the treatment gold standard for many mental health disorders, including anxiety. Self-guided CBT is most effective, however, when it focuses not only on replacing distorted thought patterns, but making *behavioral changes* that align with new beliefs.
- Identify your cognitive distortions, drill healthier alternatives, and notice if this changes how you feel. Then, make the shift concrete by taking one small action step that aligns with your new perspective. Remember that change has to include thoughts, feelings, *and* behaviors to be truly effective.
- Metacognition is the ability to think about the way you're thinking. By focusing not on the content of our overthinking, but on our beliefs about overthinking itself, we can make high-level changes.
- CBT typically targets thoughts about the world, whereas MCT targets our thoughts about thinking, whether positive

(overthinking helps the problem) or negative (overthinking is a problem).

- Moving out from the *content* level and into the *metacognitive* level is often a powerful way to start shifting the long-held thought patterns that are keeping you feeling stuck. Pay attention to your "worry rules" and be honest about the effect they have on you. By gently challenging these rules with targeted experiments, we can start to make lasting changes.
- The "transdiagnostic" approach is about looking beyond specific symptoms and investigating the underlying *processes* and *mechanisms* that are common to *all* mental health disorders. This way, we can use a single Unified Protocol to address a wide range of symptoms at once.
- We can learn about how our overthinking functions and how it maintains our anxiety. Identify your safety-seeking behaviors and experiment with reducing them by just 10% at first. When we *approach*, *act,* and *turn outwards*, we replace old mechanisms with new, healthier ones. Just notice your urge, then gently do the "opposite move." Talk kindly to yourself as you go.

Chapter Five – Acceptance and Action

Our final chapter concerns the deepest and possibly most effective mindset shifts we can make when it comes to anxious overthinking.

Here, we'll consider the **paradoxical magic of *accepting* our anxiety**, and what that actually means, moment to moment. We'll investigate why meditation isn't always the best option for overthinkers, and how you can tailor your mindfulness approach so it genuinely brings more peace and groundedness into your life.

Finally, we'll finish with one of the **most powerful remedies for anxiety**. It's not a psychological theory, a philosophical approach, a clever method, trick, or technique.

It's **action**.

And we can start taking conscious, meaningful action in the right direction *today*, one small and easy step at a time.

Stop trying to "fix" anxiety. Instead, start accepting it

"Don't seek for everything to happen as you wish it would, but rather wish that everything happens as it actually will—then your life will flow well.

-   Epictetus

Big idea: Sometimes, the thing that most reliably relieves anxiety is to stop trying to force a solution in the first place. With acceptance, we drop the endless struggle to FIX and stop seeing our immediate experience as a problem to solve.

A strange thing can happen when overthinkers start trying to face their fears rather than avoid them.

They bravely shift the focus of their attention, turn towards their fears... and immediately go into aggressive "fix up mode."

If you're an overthinker, you'll be more than familiar with this phenomenon!

Fix up mode = the belief that "I must get rid of this feeling, thought, or condition before I can live and be well."

Fix up mode is what makes you rush in to find solutions, to solve problems once and for all, and to finally get away from that awful thing that's holding you back.

This belief runs _deep_. It's built into our mental problem/solution architecture—we think of ourselves as "before" people and yearn to be those happy, relaxed "after" people we know we should be.

The only thing standing in the way?

- This awful feeling you have.
- These stressful and crazy thoughts.
- This stupid anxiety disorder.
- This useless personality.
- This broken brain.
- This messy, incomplete, imperfect, and awkward place you're in right now...

And so, when an anxious overthinker attempts to "get better," it's often just code for, "fix myself up so I can be OK again."

When we say "self-improvement" or "healing," what we sometimes mean is "I cannot accept myself or my life, so I'm going to fix it all so I don't have to feel bad anymore."

The impulse to remove the bad thing is only natural, but the paradox is that it traps us in a present moment that always feels *lacking*. Wrong. Broken.

In other words, a problem to solve.

And it's ironically *this* attitude that keeps us feeling anxious and unhappy.

You cannot grow and develop from a place of self-hate.

You cannot judge and condemn yourself into feeling OK.

And you cannot force yourself to be calm, content, and grounded.

Analogy: The "Chinese finger puzzle" is an unassuming, flexible tube into which you to stick your index fingers. When you pull to remove your fingers, however, the tube tightens up and holds you trapped.

The more you pull, the tighter the tube and the more firmly trapped you become.

You only solve the puzzle when you do the *opposite* of what you think will help—stop pulling. When you stop, the tube loosens, and your fingers come out. Easily.

This parallels how **acceptance is a way to solve problems by abandoning the effort to solve problems**. By shifting into acceptance mode and out of anxious fix-up mode, we find more calm and ease… and quite possibly a real solution to our problems.

- A study published in the *Journal of Consulting and Clinical Psychology* investigated whether people diagnosed with GAD would benefit from a program of acceptance-based behavioral therapy.
- This therapy focused on **"increasing acceptance** of internal experiences and encouraging action in valued domains."
- After treatment, participants showed significant reductions in their symptoms—and that improvement was still there at a 3- and 9-month follow-up.

- In fact, 78% of participants no longer even met the criteria for GAD (Roemer et. al., 2008).

The authors conclude that **acceptance-based therapy works because it targets experiential avoidance**.

So, what exactly is the experience we are avoiding?

- Painful thoughts
- Painful feelings
- Painful memories
- Painful physical sensations

The avoidance comes when we try to:

- Escape
- Suppress
- Ignore
- Resist
- "Fix"

Experiential avoidance works, but it doesn't work well, and it doesn't work for long.

The belief is that uncomfortable experiences are intolerable, so we need to take control and deal with those experiences somehow.

Experiential avoidance can take many forms—including disguising itself as something rational and helpful, like:

- Overworking and keeping busy, such as compulsive cleaning.
- Using substances, drinking, or overeating.

- Distraction or denial.
- Ignoring certain topics or just refusing to engage.
- "Toxic positivity" and reassurance.
- Procrastinating tasks or zoning out during hard conversations.
- A vigorous "fix up" project.

Experiential avoidance → anxiety.

Acceptance → peace.

One of the biggest traps that overthinkers can fall into is a trap of our own making: We tell ourselves that we're fixing ourselves up, finding solutions to problems, healing, getting treatment, and engaging in personal development.

Meanwhile, all of this may conceal what we're *really* doing—plain old experiential avoidance!

How to drop the struggle

Escaping or avoiding the source of your anxiety only worsens the anxiety in the long run.

On the other hand, you don't have to "embrace" your anxiety, dwell on it, or make permanent best friends with it, either!

Instead, there's a quieter, calmer place somewhere between these two extremes. Here, we just **make room** for what we're actually feeling.

No more, no less.

Analogy: A guest turns up at your home uninvited. You don't really like this guest (they're rude and difficult and stress you out) but they're not going to leave so you let them come in and sit at the table.

You don't waste energy having a fight with them, but you also don't go out of your way to engage in conversation. You don't argue, explain, negotiate, beg, apologize, defend yourself, or get angry.

You're polite, and when they speak, you listen. But they're *definitely* not calling the shots in your home, and besides, you have other guests at the table that you *have* invited—these guests are fun, inspirational, and encouraging, and you love having them over so you can make plans together.

➜ Acceptance is not about what you do, but the *attitude* you hold.

"I don't like this guest much, but he's here now and it's not a problem. I don't have to rush to do anything just because he arrived. There is no big emergency. He'll go when he wants to, and that's fine too. In the meantime, I'll enjoy my other guests."

Acceptance means treating your unwanted experiences in just the same way.

Step 1: Detach

Just because an uncomfortable or unwanted sensation has shown up in your field of awareness, it doesn't mean that you have to respond to it. Give the right name to what's going on:

"This is discomfort, not a problem to solve."

The discomfort is:

- Not a command
- Not a demand
- Not an emergency
- Not a compulsion
- Not an outstanding situation that requires resolution

It's just discomfort. And it can just sit there at the table.

Unpleasant? Yes.

Unwanted? Definitely.

But it just is what it is. And it is relieving to know that you don't have to make it more than it is!

Step 2: "Allow + rejoin"

Just like with the Chinese finger puzzle, sometimes our anxiety comes from our very attempts to get rid of it.

Instead, practice *allowing*.

It's easier, more relaxed, and conserves your energy.

➜ Remember: The uncomfortable sensation is here with you, *whether you like it or not.* Experiential avoidance does precisely nothing to change the reality of that experience. So why waste energy on it?

If your unwanted guest is going to be there one way or another, then the easiest way through is to simply *allow* him to be there—and let go of the waste and stress of trying to fight against his existence.

- Just **notice the experience that you are having.** Be aware of all the feelings that come with it. Maybe that's a retelling of the familiar old worst-case-scenario story, or a sensation of tightness in the chest, or a feeling of uneasiness.
- **Breathe normally, and just be here,** with yourself, as you are. You have nowhere to go. There's no outstanding task to attend to. No problem to solve. Just make some room for the experience you're having.
  - You don't need to calm yourself.
  - You don't need to decide whether you're right or wrong, reasonable or unreasonable, allowed or not allowed.
  - You don't need to pretend that the situation is something that it isn't.
  - You don't need to think of a solution or a way out.
  - You don't have to be strong or wise or insightful or good.
  - You don't need to make a judgment or decide whether you like what's happening.
  - You don't need to analyze or understand anything.
  - You don't need to rank or evaluate the experience.
- When you've made some room for the experience as it is, without avoidance, then

choose to **rejoin life** with one small action you'd do if you weren't stuck.

- ○ Connect with your other guests and remind yourself of the plans and projects you had with them—that means refocusing on your values and goals.
- ○ Whether you reach out to a loved one, take a step on a meaningful task, or just get up and walk to the mailbox, you're removing focus from the unwanted experience *without going into avoidance.*

The wonderful thing about accepting your experience rather than avoiding it is how often it actually gets things moving again. Your fingers release easily out of the Chinese finger puzzle, so to speak.

Often, when we drop the struggle against discomfort, we realize that 90% of the discomfort *was* the struggle! And by plainly accepting what is real for us, we may discover new solutions, fresh possibilities, or alternative ways forward that we never considered before.

Sometimes, the unwanted guest speaks up and tells us something that is genuinely interesting. We didn't invite him and we hated having him over... but didn't he have a useful message to share, in the end?

Mindfulness meditation for chronic overthinking

"In aimlessness, we see that we do not lack anything, that we already are what we want to become, and our striving just comes to a halt. We are at peace in

the present moment... Aimlessness and nirvana are one."

-   Tich Nhat Hanh

Big idea: Mindfulness and meditation *can* be helpful for overthinkers. Done incorrectly, however, it can backfire and intensify anxiety. To make mindfulness meditation safe for over-busy minds, we need to make some important tweaks and adjustments.

Much guidance for anxious overthinkers *begins* with a suggestion to be more mindful and meditate. But in this book we have saved mindfulness for the *end*, and perhaps you can guess why.

Without a full understanding of what anxiety is and how it functions in your life, it's easy to fall into the **trap of mindfulness-as-rumination.**

Like other techniques and approaches we've discussed so far, mindfulness is a tool—and a tool can be used or misused.

It's not that there is anything wrong with mindfulness, or that its principles are unsound; rather, anxious minds may be a little more ready to misinterpret and misapply certain directives—without realizing it.

- **Inward focus** – most mindfulness techniques encourage inward, self-referential thought and a kind of introspection. For overthinkers, this can actually exacerbate the problem and create more psychological strain.

- **Poorly processed trauma** – focusing intently on inner experiences may accidentally trigger traumatic memories and worsen panic.
- **Emotional blunting** – some mindfulness techniques encourage a kind of prolonged detachment that can lead to numbness and apathy.
- **"Spiritual bypassing"** – overthinkers can sometimes use meditation principles and concepts to avoid and neutralize their true feelings. Both intellectualization and "spiritualization" can become safety-seeking behaviors.

Finally, there is one especially common mindfulness pitfall for overthinkers, and it looks like this:

"I must do this perfectly" → mental force and effort → "failure" → self-judgment.

This "trying too hard" loop merely becomes one more thread of anxious overthinking, meaning you start to overthink your inability to stop overthinking!

There is plenty of credible research to suggest that mindfulness (often "mindfulness-based stress reduction" or MBSR) is helpful for reducing worry and anxiety symptoms (Hoge et. al., 2013; Golden & Gross, 2014; Bhattacharya & Hofmann, 2023).

However, we should exercise care, as mindfulness is not one-size-fits-all.

How to make mindfulness work for you

As we have seen, overthinkers benefit from:

- Grounding in the concrete
- Cognitive defusion
- Turning attention outwards
- Approach rather than avoidance
- Refocusing on values and action
- Acceptance and "making room"

Mindfulness and meditation techniques that are in alignment with this will be extremely beneficial for an overthinker. For example:

- **Choose guided meditations** that provide structure and movement over free-form protocols that encourage "just sitting." Remember that ambiguity and abstraction can be major triggers!
- **Choose exercises that encourage gentle detachment from thoughts** rather than "emptying your mind." The idea is not to stop or control thought, but to allow thoughts to arise and pass again without you having to analyze, judge, or fix anything.
- **Choose techniques that focus on externalities, action, and movement** rather than those that have you sit still and introspect. You can be supremely mindful while walking, doing chores, practicing yoga, or even dancing or playing sports. Think

about *immersion and focus* rather than *stillness.*

- **Choose sensory and embodied engagement** over mental activity. It can be difficult to "turn the mind off," but it's easier to switch focus onto sensory or bodily processing. This "channel" of experience is slower, more comfortable, and more rooted in the present.

For many overthinkers, meditation and mindfulness take a little bit of practice—and they often have to let go of what they think their experience *should* be, and work directly with what it really *is*.

If you're just getting started with mindfulness, here are a few things to try.

Tip 1: "Return reps" meditation

It can be stressful and intimidating thinking of meditation as something you have to *do*… and, therefore, do incorrectly. Especially for those of us with perfectionist tendencies, it can get really frustrating to repeatedly notice your mind wandering.

Judgment and self-criticism creep in.

Soon, meditation feels like a chore, or worse—a punishment.

Turn this all around by reframing your task entirely. Tell yourself that your only goal (if you can even call it that) is to gently and quietly label what your thoughts are doing, moment to moment.

Of course, now and then your mind will wander and you'll forget what you're doing and start thinking of something else.

THAT'S OK!

Tell yourself that *there really isn't any way to do it wrong.* Whether your mind stays on task or whether it wanders doesn't matter, because your "job" is to simply watch it do what it's doing.

Even if your mind wanders off a hundred times in a minute, if it comes back 101 times, note it and carry on. You're still meditating. You're still "doing it right."

Practice this "return rep" style meditation for just 5 or 10 minutes at a time. Even a minute squeezed into the day here and there will have an impact.

Tip 2: Body-scan interrupt

You are not just what's happening inside your head. You are also your body!

A body scan meditation is a great way to quickly shift out of "storytelling mode" and into "sensory mode." You are still being mindful—but your awareness is now embodied and anchored into the present—which is, after all, the only place your body can ever be.

Try to notice sensations without judging, categorizing, fixing, or telling a story about them.

Imagine that your conscious awareness is a beam of light that you shine on different parts of your body.

Move attention slowly from forehead → jaw → chest → belly → hands → feet... the direction or order is not important. The attention you bring *is*.

Tip 3: Mindful single-tasking

You don't have to have a formal meditation practice—the day is filled with opportunities to pause, unhook from runaway thoughts, and re-ground.

➜   There are as many mindfulness windows as there are moments—an infinite and infinitely renewing number!

One easy way to counter anxious overthinking with mindful presence is to simply... be present with whatever it is you're doing. You don't have to wait until your chores are done before you can sit down and do a mindfulness exercise; instead, do those chores but do them with full sensory attention.

Don't just wash the dishes; fully engross yourself in every sensation that comes with the warm water, the texture of the smooth ceramic plate, the contrast between wet and dry... try to picture that the brain in your head is switched off, and that all your awareness is now in your fingertips.

When (not if!) your mind starts to spin out, label it "thinking" and return to the task at hand. Return to those soap bubbles. Return to that faint pink and green swirl of color on the soap bubble. Come back and wash the dishes with everything you have.

You can do *any* activity this way. Try:

- Finding a peaceful moment while showering.
- An "eating meditation" at meals.
- Moving with alertness and presence through a sequence of stretches.
- Focusing 100% on the task of cooking, cleaning, dressing, driving, writing, or just taking out the trash.

Mindfulness works best when it follows a **"little and often"** pattern. The more mindful you are in ordinary, everyday situations, the greater your awareness and the easier you'll find it to self-regulate, moment to moment.

Tip 4: Transition to action

Meditation is rightly understood as "goal-less" but that doesn't mean you can't incorporate it intentionally into the rest of your daily routine.

After a mindfulness exercise, from that renewed place of stillness and awareness, ask yourself:

- "What unmet needs am I aware of right now?"
- "What is the next move I'd like to make?"
- "Where would I like my attention to go now?"
- "How can I take healthful and beneficial action right now?"

Meditation can act like a reset—and from that reset position, we can take a breath and move forward with purpose and clarity.

Pause. Accept. *Then* act.

Remember: You can be anxious *and* mindful.

Serenely encounter reality. And if your reality is that you are not serene, then encounter that lack of serenity *with* serenity!

Your goal is never to achieve some perfect end state. Your goal is not to be "good." You are just here.

And that's enough.

(Finally, one important thing to remember: you don't *have to* meditate. Mindfulness and meditation can be extremely useful, but they are just tools. You will not be missing out on anything if you decide that you'd prefer to use other tools).

Break overthinking with behavioral activation

"Do what you can, with what you have, where you are."

-       *Theodore Roosevelt*

Big idea: Overthinking is fed by excessive introspection. Break this cycle of passivity and withdrawal by re-engaging with the outside world. The solution to overthinking is not more thinking—it's mindful, meaningful action.

On the road to recovery, there can be strange moment when one almost wonders, "What am I going to do now if not overthink?"

Overthinking is often *under-doing* in disguise.

The irony is that as our minds start to quieten down, it may dawn on us just how much time and energy we had previously sacrificed to rumination, looping, and endless analysis.

The feeling of emerging from the world of thinking into the world of doing can be exhilarating—and a little strange!

"Behavioral activation" or BA is a helpful framework to lean on here, even though it's traditionally used to treat depression.

The core principles of this therapeutic model are simple:

- **Action precedes motivation.**
- **Motivation isn't necessary.** We don't need to wait till we feel better to act; if we act (even if we don't entirely "feel it") it will eventually lead to changes in thoughts and feelings.
- Withdrawal and avoidance worsen the problem, but we can change everything by approaching and engaging.
- **Our environment can provide reinforcement.** The more we engage, the better we feel, and the more we *want* to engage.

If you're a habitual overthinker, you more or less "live in your head."

The trouble with that is that your own thoughts, feelings, and interpretations have nothing to feed on except themselves. They twist in on themselves in self-referential spirals, and there is nothing to challenge or push against them. Those loops tighten and become stranger, more anxious, and less anchored in reality.

However, if you **turn outwards and actively engage with the world**, it's as though you bring some fresh air into the stale room of your mind.

By interacting with your external environment, you begin to have a more balanced, more realistic "conversation" with reality compared to the one you may ordinarily have in the privacy of your own mind.

You establish *healthy* loops:

You step outside of your head and engage → you feel pleasure and reward → you want to do more.

You have not just reduced rumination, you've increased functional, adaptive, and meaningful action. You have replaced an unhealthy coping mechanism with a valuable life skill that will give you the chance at creating a life you actually want to live.

The answer to the question, "What am I going to do now if not overthink?" then becomes, "You're going to get out there and LIVE!"

Too many overthinkers get trapped in solutions that are really just more of the same problem in disguise:

- Introspective talk therapy
- Self-analysis
- Meditation, journalling, endless contemplation
- Passive withdrawal (yes, even if it's called "self-care"!)

The real solution may lie in precisely the opposite direction.

Instead of retreating into our own mental worlds, BA asks us to connect meaningfully with the real world around us. The goal is to work from the outside in, and re-anchor yourself to your world in ways that are genuinely fulfilling.

Broadly, the process is as follows:

- **Initial assessment:** How are you currently spending your time? Honestly track your daily activities as well as your overall mood levels.
- **Reconnect to values and goals:** Overthinking poses as a solution but usually takes us further away from the things we actually care about. What you do stems from what you care about, so take the time to clarify what those things actually are.
- **Make a plan:** Instead of passive overthinking, actively construct a schedule where you progressively attempt small activities in line with your values.

- **Review your progress:** After some time, assess your schedule and your mood levels. What's worked?

There is evidence that BA is at least as effective as CBT (McIndoo et. al., 2016), especially when combined with elements of mindfulness practice.

Present moment awareness and acceptance + meaningful action = a powerful combo!

How to be your own behavioral activation coach

Though a trained mental health professional can certainly walk you through the process, you can easily apply BA principles to your own life, right now.

At this point in the book, you should have a growing ability to recognize and label overthinking when it appears. To practice BA properly, **stay alert, stay active, and stay grounded**.

A few principles to remember:

- **Just do it.** There will never be a "right time" to start, you don't need permission or approval, there is nobody coming to rescue you or do it for you, and you don't have to delay until you're feeling positive or motivated. Action *first*—emotion follows. You can be anxious and still act. You can be doubtful and still act. "Ready" is a conscious decision—not a feeling.
- **Life is not what you think and feel—it's what you do.** Impact matters more than

intent. Daniel Kahneman once said, "Nothing in life is as important as you think it is while you are thinking about it." Don't be a philosopher—be a scientist and go out there and *test* your ideas.

- **Take the step into life.** It's not entirely true that "knowledge is power." Instead, as Tony Robbins says, "Knowledge is only potential power. Action is power." Thoughts are just electrochemical events in the brain. But action is what changes our world. Action is what connects us to other people. And action is what shapes our identity according to our values.

Step 1: Do an honest activity appraisal

As an overthinker, you may feel "busy"—but that activity might be inside your head alone, while your actual life is marked by inaction.

➜ For a week or two, track how you are actually spending your time, day to day, hour to hour, minute to minute. What are you DOING with your life, in a very practical sense?
➜ At the same time, keep track of how you FEEL.

Draw up a spreadsheet or keep a log where you note down exactly what you're doing (*not* thinking) every waking hour of the day, and your overall mood level, say out of ten.

After a week or two is over, have a look at your data.

- Tally up how many hours you spend working, watching TV, going to the gym, spending time with family, playing computer games, etc.
- You might like to create a pie chart to see the relative proportions.
- See if you can identify any patterns and connections between activities and how you feel. What are you doing when your mood is the highest or lowest? What activities tend to come before mood changes?

Step 2: Explore your values and goals

The next step is to carefully consider who or what matters most to you.

The reason for this step is obvious: Action is good, but not just any old action will do! Action *that is in alignment with values* is what moves your life forward and makes it satisfying.

You don't need to overthink it, though. Just become curious:

- When did I feel proudest/happiest/most fulfilled in life? What was I doing?
- Who do I admire most and why?
- On the other hand, who do I judge or condemn, and why?
- If money was no object, what would I do with myself?
- If other people's expectations and opinions didn't matter, what would I do with myself?
- The times I felt worst in my life, what was missing?
- What would my perfect day look like?

- What would I want my obituary to say about me?
- If I had one lesson to teach everyone, what would it be?

These questions can point you to the things that really matter to you.

The next part is the most interesting:

→ How do your findings in step 1 compare to the values you've uncovered?
→ Are you actually living the kind of life that someone with your values would live?

For example, you may notice that even though you value simplicity, sincerity, and calm, you spend exactly zero hours every week doing anything that could be called simple, sincere, or calm!

You may *say* that you value family time, for example, but when you tally up what you actually *do* each week, you spend ten times as many hours gaming, scrolling, and reading online news articles that rile you up.

Step 3: Make a plan and schedule action

Even if what you discovered in steps 1 and 2 wasn't all that encouraging, don't worry—you're on the right path.

The next thing to do is gradually introduce value-aligned mini-actions into your daily schedule. In previous chapters, we explored the power of taking any action to get out of your head—go for a walk, **do** a grounding exercise or reach out to a friend, for example.

With BA, however, your activities are a little more *targeted* and speak directly to your values and goals.

➜ In effect, you are addressing overthinking by slowly *replacing* it. You swap out the time you'd spend looping and spiraling with real-world activities that actually make you feel good.

IMPORTANT: The goal is not to give yourself a new life overnight or accomplish impressive feats.

All you're doing is *starting*.

Let momentum build.

The truth is that at first, you probably won't feel like doing these activities. Your mind will tell you that they're boring, uncomfortable, stupid, or unlikely to make a real difference. Guess what? You don't have to argue with these thoughts.

Because remember: *Action precedes emotion*. Act even if you don' feel motivated to do so! When you act, you start up a relationship with your environment, and that environment in turn *acts on you*.

In time, you'll find these activities a little more rewarding, and you'll want to do them more. But the initial goal isn't to create good feelings. It's just to get started.

Example: Let's say you've identified certain values around service, protecting the environment, and community. You decide that a good action would be to pick up litter in your neighborhood. You make a plan to carry a small plastic bag with you so you can pick up litter whenever you see it while out walking. You schedule this for three nights a week, at 7 p.m. during your after-dinner walk—thirty minutes in total.

IMPORTANT: Continue to track what you're doing day-to-day, and how you feel.

Step 3: Practice the "two-minute starter rule"

BA takes time.

It takes patience and commitment.

But it's the small, gradual changes that end up making the most impactful and lasting difference.

- At first, you may not want to do your scheduled activities. That's OK. This is simply inertia and it's normal. Agree with yourself that when the scheduled time comes, you'll start and *do just two minutes.*
  - Usually, once you're over that two-minute hump, you're more willing to continue.
- If you find yourself overthinking and spiraling at some other point in your daily routine, remember these mini-tasks and try one there and then—even if it's just for two minutes. It might not be 7 p.m., but if you're

feeling strung out, step outside for a quick walk to pick up some litter.

○ Overthinking often collapses in the face of movement. Don't argue with yourself, make excuses, feel guilty, analyze things, or start telling a story about why you've failed. It's all irrelevant—just get out of our head entirely and connect to an action you already know has value.

Step 4: Reflect

After a few weeks of taking value-driven mini-actions, you should have some data:

- What you did
- How you felt

You've introduced some new activity, now is your chance to see what these behaviors have "activated" in you.

- Has your overall mood changed?
- How often did you manage to achieve the mini-activities you scheduled?
- In general, how do you feel after taking values-driven action? How does this compare to what you *predicted* you'd feel at the time?

Over time, you will see your life slowly changing before your eyes—there is less and less time spent passively ruminating, and more and more time spent in active engagement. What's more, you should be able to see that (despite your grumpy, anxious brain predicting otherwise) taking action genuinely *feels better.*

➜ The old dogma says: "Overthinking is useful. I *have to* overthink. Overthinking is what keeps me safe and sane and feeling OK."

But if you follow the BA protocol for a few weeks or months, you'll actually prove to yourself that this is just not true! The more you act, the better you feel—whether you're motivated at the time or not.

The next time your brain says, "Hey, stay here and ruminate with me. Withdraw a little and let's churn over this old idea one more time," you will *know* that that path ultimately won't make you feel good.

And you will *know* that getting up to do something active will make you feel better, because you've already proved it to yourself.

What "action" is... and isn't

Before we conclude, let's explore a sneaky trap that sometimes catches overthinkers.

Take a look at some of these mini-activities:

- Rework my essay
- Go over the vacation plan
- Prepare for the meeting tomorrow
- Tweak that email
- Research more about XYZ
- Make a plan for the weekend
- Rehearse what I'll say to my mother-in-law

- Review the budget
- Work on my job-hunting strategy

Looks fine, right?

Revising, preparing, reviewing… it's true that anticipating and preparing for the future is a natural and healthy function of the mind.

The trouble is that some of us can be ultra-productive and organized people… but then we just *keep going* until those same mental processes lead to analysis paralysis, immobilizing perfectionism, indecision, and panic.

For some of us, these "actions" are dangerously close to becoming "overthinking."

The trouble is that **we can disguise rumination and overthinking as action**, and fool ourselves that endless rehearsal, research, and planning counts as "doing" something.

Without knowing it, we cross the line from "doing" into "thinking"… and then into "overthinking."

Where is that line? What is the difference between planning and overthinking?

Healthy planning and preparation is:

- Constructive
- Time-limited
- Action-oriented
- Focused on possible solutions

Plain old overthinking is:

- Anxiety-driven
- Unending, repetitive, looping
- Passive; a (poor) substitute for action
- Focused on worst-case scenarios

The biggest difference?

Healthy planning is ACTION, or else it leads to ACTION.

Overthinking is never true action, and all it leads to is more overthinking.

- Are you creating a clear path to action?
- Have you got a clearly defined endpoint (a way to know when your action is accomplished)?
- Is your thinking *going* anywhere (towards action)?

If not, then you may no longer be planning, but overthinking.

When considering BA as a method for overcoming overthinking, we need to be honest about any tendency to get stuck in the weeds of rehearsal, reviewing, planning, "researching," etc.

It's tempting to avoid taking real action by escaping into busywork that *looks like* it's accomplishing something but is really just more avoidance.

If this sounds like you, don't worry. There are plenty of simple ways to keep yourself action-oriented and focused.

- **Drill the "done is better than perfect" motto.** Imperfect action beats perfect action that somehow never materializes. Stop seeing perfectionism as a high standard and start seeing it as an obstacle getting in your way. Instead of "Is this perfect?" ask, "What is the next step in the process?"

- **Set time limits for yourself.** There is a place in life for rehearsing, planning, researching, preparing, etc. But these things are best in small doses. Allow yourself to review and plan, but for an allocated time only. Stay focused. Set the timer then stop when it goes off. Your thoughts should all point towards the same thing: What are you going to *do* with all this analysis?

- **What can you control?** You can't predict every outcome, and you certainly can't control every outcome. Narrow your focus down to those things that you can reasonably influence and find the discipline to set aside the rest.

- **Just start.** Planning and research are the world's most sophisticated avoidance strategies because they really do seem productive—you can even fool yourself that you're making progress! But remind yourself that you "don't have to see the whole staircase to take the first step." Let your planning focus on the next right step, that's all.

Overthinking that is based on rehearsal and preparation is thinking that circles *around* the discomfort of uncertainty, without ever facing it.

It's safety-seeking behavior:

- "If I can perfectly predict the future, then I can control it, and I can be safe."
- "A scary thing might be coming. But I can out-think it."
- "If I start, it's possible I'll fail. So I won't start just yet. Instead, I'll delay and think of ways to guarantee a good outcome."

We need to notice this tendency in ourselves and consistently push against it, so that we are cultivating a "bias for action" rather than a tendency to avoid, escape, or control.

ACTION is one of the purest and most effective antidotes to overthinking.

Are you trapped in planning, rehearsing, reviewing, revising…?

Pause.

Become aware.

Then push yourself to take just one tiny active step in the right direction.

Overthinking is a habit, and habits have their own momentum.

- The more you overthink, the more you'll want to overthink.

- The more you withdraw, the easier it will be to keep withdrawing.
- The less you act, the harder it will feel to act.

BA is not magic; it's just about turning the tide in the other direction. It's about giving yourself the chance to build up momentum in the other direction.

Author Brad Stulberg says, "We think our being influences our doing but it's often the other way around. ... Show up and take action on the things that matter to you and see if your thinking and feeling follow."

Ask yourself:

Who do I want to be in this life?

What does a person like that do?

Then go and do that.

Summary:

- Sometimes, the thing that most reliably relieves anxiety is to stop trying to force a solution in the first place. With acceptance, we drop the endless struggle to FIX and stop seeing our immediate experience as a problem to solve. Detach, allow the feeling, then rejoin life again.
- Mindfulness and meditation *can* be helpful for overthinkers. Done incorrectly, however, they can backfire and actually intensify anxiety.

- Guided mediations, sensory engagement, defusion techniques, and embodied mindfulness techniques are great for overthinkers. You can also try body scans or "mindful single-tasking" moments throughout the day to build awareness without triggering overthinking.
- Overthinking is fed by excessive introspection. Break this cycle of passivity and withdrawal by re-engaging with the outside world. The solution to overthinking is not more thinking—it's mindful, meaningful action.
- Overthinking is sometimes under-doing. Behavioral activation sees that action precedes emotion and encourages us to re-engage meaningfully with our environment through action. We feel a sense of reward and fulfilment, then want to act again.
- Honestly appraise your current activity habits, revisit your values and goals, and then schedule mini activities to start building momentum. Watch out for rumination disguised as action, such as planning, research, etc. Give yourself a time limit, then just start with one small action you can control. Done is better than perfect.

Conclusion

Even if overthinking has played a major role in your life so far, now is the perfect time to start making changes in the right direction. Even if you're not perfectly convinced yet. Even if you've struggled to make progress before.

Remember that recovery doesn't happen all at once; rather, it's the tiny, almost-invisible daily changes that make all the difference in the long-run.

If overthinking is a habit, then it is overcome by a greater habit: the consistent decision, moment by moment, to *not* let anxiety be the driving force in your life.

Well done for making it to the end of this book. And well done for all the positive changes you're going to carry with you into the future.

The next time you find yourself spiraling, remember that you can come back to these pages and to the gentler, more balanced, and more grounded thoughts they contain:

- My thoughts are not dangerous.
- My feelings are not dangerous.

- My physical sensations and perceptions are not dangerous.
- I don't like experiencing anxiety, but it's OK that I am experiencing it.
- These sensations are normal. I don't have to react.
- I'm safe, even if it doesn't feel like it right now.
- This experience is temporary.
- I can live a good and meaningful life even if I sometimes feel anxious.
- I can steer my mind. I can change the story I tell.
- No matter what, I can take small action steps, even if I'm uncomfortable.
- I can handle not knowing. It's not a problem. It's not an emergency.
- My brain may tell me that something is important, urgent, or dangerous, but that doesn't necessarily mean it *is*.
- No matter what, there is always something I can control. I can choose to focus on that.
- Even if I 100% believe in my anxious thought right now, I could be 100% wrong, because I've been wrong before.
- I have been in challenging situations before, and I have coped.
- Challenging things happen in life. But they're usually not as bad as I predict, and I know I can handle it."
- I don't need perfect certainty to be safe/restful/OK/happy/functional.

- I am OK. I can feel unsure, incomplete, in process, or anxious, and still be OK.
- I don't have to please, accommodate, help, and prioritize other people to be safe. It's not a disaster if someone disagrees with me, is disappointed in me, or doesn't like me.
- Negative thoughts are normal. I don't have to fight them. But I can defuse from them.
- A thought is just a thought. It's not a command, a directive, a universal truth, a compulsion, or a permanent fact about my identity.
- I can stay present, I can stay open, and I can make good choices, even if my mind is racing.
- I don't have to be perfect or have everything figured out.
- This feeling is not a problem to solve. I can make room for it. It will pass.
- I can handle "I don't know."
- I'm comfortable with waiting. A delay is not a threat.
- I don't have to have all the answers to make a good decision now or take the next right step. I can figure things out as I go.
- This is a process. Today I'll engage with today's business, and I'll deal with tomorrow's business tomorrow.
- I'm not always in complete control, and I don't need to be to feel safe.
- I don't need to predict the future to be well-prepared for it. I can do my best in this moment, and that is enough.

- I can rest, even if there are still some things unresolved in my world.
- **I'M OK. Right now, just as I am.**

Overthinkers have a secret superpower: Once they truly understand their minds, accept them, and learn to *channel* all that brainpower in the right direction, life quickly starts to shift.

Just be aware.

Stay with the feeling, label it, accept it.

Focus on what you can control, on what matters, and then act accordingly.

Tell yourself again and again that at the end of the day, it doesn't really matter what's going on inside your head. **What matters is what you choose to do next.**